SHORT RIDES

SHORT RIDES

by Wendy Borgstrom

Boston ♦ Lace Publications
an imprint of Alyson Publications, Inc.

Typeset and printed in the United States of America.

This is a paperback original from Lace Publications,
an imprint of Alyson Publications, Inc., 40 Plympton St., Boston, Mass. 02118.
Distributed in England by GMP Publishers,
P.O. Box 247, London N17 9QR, England.

This book is printed on acid-free, recycled paper.

First edition, first printing: June 1992

5 4 3 2 1

ISBN 1-55583-313-6

Editing and proofreading: Tina Portillo

Dedicated to Flory, Wooley, and Jude
with much love

Contents

Her

I

The door banged shut, jangling my nerves as I yanked it, a little too hard, behind me. I always felt so mixed up when I left her office. Part of me wanted to run away, and part of me wanted very much to stay — to stay there in her loving presence where she could take care of me for eternity.

There was another feeling too — a strange, dual sort of desire. Sometimes it was a desire to please her, to be the kind of person she would approve of. Other times, in my deepest and most daring fantasies, the desire was sexual; usually that part came out only in dreams. The conscious thought of making love with her, though tantalizing, made me shudder with fear and self-reproach. I couldn't help but feel there was something wrong, maybe even perverse, about having these kinds of thoughts about her.

When I exited the building a cold winter wind snapped at me. I pulled my collar up and bent my head down against it. Nervous excitement still twitched inside me, but the chill helped to clear my head. Snatches of the previous hour's conversation ran through my brain. I needed coffee and a warm place to sit so I could try to sort it all out. I went into the coffee shop at the end of the block. There, I could separate myself just enough to think, while remaining just a little connected to her by the proximity of the place to her office.

I sat down at a little table in a corner of the shop so that I could be as private as possible. As the hot coffee ran down my throat I began to relax. Now I could sift through the pieces of the last hour, and find one to latch onto and dwell upon.

Out of nowhere, she had asked me about my fantasies. She wanted me to tell her, just like that, all about my secret inner life. There I was fairly calm, sitting back in the big stuffed chair rambling on about some pretty mundane stuff. It was during these times that I would study and absorb her being, as she listened quietly.

I'd examine the surroundings: her desk and chair, her artwork on the walls, the rug. I noted every detail about her clothing, the way she sat, her hair, her facial expressions. I was always particularly attuned to her face, watching for any betrayal of her true feelings. With one movement of an eyebrow or a lip, she would unknowingly assure me that she cared deeply for me or show me her displeasure. I loved it when I made her laugh. She would never tell me how she felt; I had to guess. When I asked, she'd focus on my asking; and when I guessed, she'd say I was projecting. So I was forced to watch for little, subtle giveaways.

Today, I had said something about fantasies. I didn't particularly want her to pick up on it. I was trying to be as open and honest as I could, knowing that was what she wanted from me. But I had learned to tell her a lot, always managing, of course, to keep stuffed away the secret, scary things.

Anyway, I was saying, "Sometimes I have this fantasy that I save the lives of a bunch of people who are in a fire or accident or something like that — that I'm the hero, you know?" I laughed to show her how silly I thought it was.

She didn't laugh but simply said, "Tell me more about your fantasies."

I was stunned, and caught off guard. I knew that if I did tell her, I'd have to be truthful; after all, there was no point in being there if I was going to make things up. I sat, quaking, trying to think of some real fantasy that didn't involve her. But as I strained my mind, I realized that all of my most important musings were about her.

So I hemmed and hawed, made a joke. She smiled only slightly, determined. Her eyes were riveted on me as I squirmed in my seat, trying desperately to come up with an acceptable fantasy. Then she dropped the bomb, giving me no way out: "Do you have fantasies about me?" She continued her close scrutiny.

I peered at her, and for a moment was convinced that she might be able to hear about my wistful longings — that she wouldn't freak out. I almost gave in and told her about the subconscious images that invaded my sleep. But when I opened my mouth something inside me said, "No! Don't tell her. Right now she looks like she can take it, but she can't." I closed my mouth.

A couple of minutes went by. "Hmm?" she said, egging me on.

"Well, most of my fantasies about you have to do with pleasing you — you know, meeting your expectations. I guess I want you to like me." Saying that wasn't easy. I hoped she would be satisfied with an admission of that caliber. But she was merciless as she searched my face carefully and then asked, "Do you have sexual fantasies about me?"

I couldn't look at her. I shifted my eyes to my lap and pretended to be thinking, but I was really trying to hide my embarrassment as I felt the blood rush to my face.

She continued to stare at me, and I felt as if I were under stage lights with a hundred pairs of eyes watching me. Gathering my resolve, I looked up at her. Her face was unchanged, without judgment: kind, interested, unrelenting.

"I don't have explicit sexual fantasies about you," I said quietly. I decided not to tell her about the dreams. "I do have sexual feelings for you, but for some reason I won't let myself think about being with you that way. Maybe it's all too threatening for me." What I had said was true. I wanted her with every fiber of my being. My dreams were certainly proof of that. But with all my might I tried to shove that desire down and would not allow myself to freely lust after her in the light of day.

She said, "Someone once said that the unconscious is less the giant tidal wave that smashes and devastates and more the quiet whimperings of a small child's ideas of truth."

"So I needn't be afraid of it, " I said, thinking out loud.

She nodded.

At any rate, whether I should have been afraid of my unconscious or not, she finally seemed satisfied to let the subject drop. She knew that mere words of reassurance weren't going to instantly make everything easier for me. After what seemed like an eternity, the session was over. I quickly took my nerve-racked, trembling body out of the office and into the freedom of the street. My mind, however, remained a prisoner of its own anguish.

Mulling over the session for about an hour in the coffee shop, I slowly grew calmer. What continued to bother me, though, was a lingering uncertainty about what I thought she thought. I was having a difficult time reading her. Usually when I left her, I was either pretty sure that she thought I was a complete jerk, or sometimes I was reasonably sure that she thought I was pretty terrific. Today, I couldn't tell at all. I suspected that I just wasn't sure how I felt about myself. Why did I have such a hard time telling her how consuming my love for her was? I had heard other people talk quite openly about being in love with their therapists; it was a common occurrence in the course of the therapeutic process. But I just couldn't quite convince myself that she wouldn't be completely grossed out if she heard me describe my deepest desires for her.

Finally I grew weary of thinking about myself and headed for home. After all, I had a whole week to work through my session before I'd have to face her again.

II

I sat up in bed, book in hand, my mind wandering. The week had flown by and tomorrow I'd see her again. I had come to a decision over the week — I was going to be completely open regarding my sexual attraction to her. I even selected a couple of not-too-hairy dreams to tell her.

I tried to imagine her response, then figured that she would betray nothing in her face. But underneath that controlled exterior I was sure that she would be very uncomfortable. She was too professional to let her real feelings show about something she knew was a difficult emotional issue for a client. And I knew I'd be too strung out to catch any subtle giveaways. Besides, I couldn't trust my own interpretations. My self-loathing around this issue was so strong, I was sure I would project some of it onto her.

I dropped off to sleep still holding onto the book.

III

I pressed the doorbell. Shortly, a buzzer went off and the lock automatically unlatched. I opened the door quickly and stepped into the waiting room. All the chairs stood empty. Good! I thought. I'm going to need these few moments of privacy to get myself together. I stood firm in my resolve to let it all hang out today.

I sat in a chair facing her closed door. From behind it came low murmurings. I hoped that the session now going on was an easy one for her, because I expected I'd wear her out during mine. Then I caught myself: Now, that is a projection, I said to myself. It's your dumb ass that's going to be on the line in there. I giggled. I was feeling kind of giddy.

I pulled a magazine from the rack so I could pretend to be reading. I had turned just a few pages when her office door swung open. Oh no, I thought, my heart quickening. I'm not ready yet!

Her previous client was a blur to me as he grabbed his coat and whisked by me. She, on the other hand, stood out clearly visible and smiled brightly, saying, "Hi, Wanda. Come on in."

I stood up stiffly, walked past her, and plunked myself down on the familiar brown stuffed chair. Gracefully she sat down across from me, leaned back, and crossed her legs.

She wore a long skirt and brown leather boots. A brightly colored silk blouse clothed her upper body. Just a hint of gold jewelry swept around her neck. Her hair, I noticed, had been recently cut, the soft brown curls complementing her feminine essence. Her large brown eyes watched me curiously, patiently; her lips were parted slightly, as if she might be getting ready to say something. But she didn't. She just looked at me and waited.

I squirmed under her gaze, trying desperately to center myself and collect my thoughts — to focus, as she had taught me. But I was so uncomfortable and my mind was so scattered and confused that I was afraid to speak, certain that my words wouldn't make any sense. I looked up at her, then down at my lap, then back up at her. There was a twinkle in her eyes, as if she knew that something was up. I looked down again.

Finally, after an immeasurable amount of time, I gathered myself up and propelled the words out of my mouth: "Remember last week when you asked me about fantasies?"

"Uh-huh," she responded, smiling slightly.

"And you wanted to know about my sexual fantasies about you?"

She said nothing but watched me quietly.

"Well, I didn't tell you everything. I didn't lie, I just left out some stuff." I paused and took a deep breath. My mind prodded me: Go ahead, just spit it out. "The truth is, I'm in love with you." There! It was done.

She sat motionless, her face alert and interested. Wasn't she supposed to say something now? She didn't, so I continued: "And yes, I do have sexual fantasies about you, mostly in dream form. I've had many sexual dreams about you. Some of them are quite explicit." I paused again. It had to be her turn now.

I was aware of a tremulousness in my body when, at last, I looked up at her and made full eye contact. Immediately I noticed her face flushing — and yes, I could swear I saw a look of pleasure. Her joyous expression captured my attention; now I couldn't take my eyes off her. It seemed as if we were fixed in a moment in time, as if someone had taken a snapshot of us.

Then her expression suddenly became serious. At first I was taken aback by this change. But the warmth around her eyes returned as she said simply, "I'm in love with you too."

I stopped breathing. Had I heard what I thought I'd heard? She spoke again: "I've never felt this way about a client before. If you hadn't brought it up, eventually I would have. It was becoming harder and harder not to tell you."

As her words fell on my ears, my mind whirled. I was utterly amazed, exhilarated — and scared. A voice amidst the swirl of emotion said: "This doesn't happen." I didn't realize I had said that out loud, but she responded, saying, "But it has."

We were silent. I was flying. Right then I felt that if nothing else good ever happened to me again, it would be all right. This was enough to satisfy me for a lifetime.

I felt a tension in the air between us, like a force drawing me toward her. She must have felt it too because she rose out of her chair and moved toward me. I rose in response. She reached out her hand and I grasped it; her touch sent a shiver through me. She pulled me close and held me, firmly yet with great tenderness.

Dizzy with delight, I was unaware of time and space. My only reality was her presence. Our bodies swayed in unison — hearts beating, breaths breathing, scents mingling. I relaxed, giving myself up to her and the present as mind and body began to meld.

Then suddenly, shrill words emanated from some place deep inside me — perhaps it was my unconscious bubbling up, using my vocal cords for its expression. I said: "Transgressing deeply rooted incest barriers."

We stood still. She stiffened, pulled back, and looked me in the eyes. A smile broadened on her lips. "What?" she asked.

"I don't know where that came from," I said. I paused, searching for an answer in her face. "Are we doing that?

Are we transgressing deeply rooted incest barriers? You know, transference and all that?"

She laughed heartily, her eyes alive and shining. She threw her arms back around me and hugged me with gusto. "You're wonderful," she chuckled.

Then she grew calm and said very seriously, "I would never do anything that I thought would hurt you. Let's just enjoy each other. There's nothing to be afraid of."

My fears were put to rest. It didn't matter anyway; something had taken me over, and it was not my intellect. She guided me over to the couch — the couch on which I would never lie during sessions, so afraid was I that uncontrollable feelings would come out. Those feelings were now laid bare, and there was no longer anything to control.

We sat facing each other and for the first time I saw all the beautiful details of her face: her smooth skin with the tiny creases around her eyes, her full lips flushed with color, her tiny nose, her one dimple that appeared when she smiled, and her remarkable penetrating brown eyes with long sensuous lashes.

A last twinge of doubt crept into my thoughts. Could she really love me? As if in answer to my question, she removed my last shred of lingering insecurity by placing her lips on mine. She kissed me lightly at first, then hard in a surge of passion. The room faded out. My heart seemed like it was trying to leap out of my chest. My ears were blocked by a loud buzzing. My genitals twitched and tingled, engorged with sensation.

We explored each other with our lips as our clothes came off. Suddenly she stopped kissing me and yanked herself an arm's length away. Her eyes, now sweetly contorted with lust, examined my body. I scanned hers. She was more beautiful than I could ever have imagined, with her round, pink curves. Softly, she stroked me, fondling me as if I were an expensive, fragile vase. Then she gently pushed me down on the couch and ran her hands all over me.

I reached up to touch her and she grabbed my hands and buried her face in them, kissing and licking the palms, sucking my fingers. Then she guided my hands over and around her breasts. Uttering a small gasp, she dropped her head and let go of my hands. She clung to the couch while I caressed her torso.

In one great surge of movement, she lifted herself up and she fell on me, quivering. The hot wind of her breath screamed in my ear.

The tingling in my groin had mounted to its edge. Slipping one sinewy thigh between mine, she spread my legs. The friction of her skin rubbing against my throbbing clit set free my long-repressed passion and I moaned, loud and low. I threw my arms above my head in a gesture of unrestrained abandonment. Her leg massaged my groin and her groin jammed into my leg. We rode and flowed, liquid from our cunts splashing over us.

With each rhythmic movement the intensity of our pulsating, surging physical love mounted, and we were lost in each other.

Soon our rocking stopped, as we shook helplessly in the blast of love ignited. Then, simultaneously, we groaned and shuddered. Sinking into each other, we lay quiet, fulfilled and floating in blissful rest.

After a while I became vaguely aware of a distant noise, like a bell. What is that? I wondered numbly. The noise got louder and louder, threatening to disrupt our peace, until finally it succeeded. "Stop that noise!" I screamed.

I awoke with a jolt. I sat straight up in my bed and a book went flying off my chest and landed, with a thump, on the floor. I looked around the room, disoriented. The alarm clock was clanging. I swatted at it in an angry frenzy, smashing it to the floor. The room became silent. The morning sun was peeking through my bedroom windows.

My mind suddenly cleared. "Damn," I said softly. *"DAMN!"*

Wind and fire

I

I splashed some cold water on my face. It felt good, even though the air conditioner was more than adequately doing its job. The terrazzo floors were cold under my bare feet as I walked across the room to the kitchen and poured myself my first cup of coffee.

The constant drone of the big boxy machine was beginning to irritate me, and even though I greatly appreciated its presence, I snapped it off. I needed to get a natural sense of my surroundings.

When I opened the front door of my small square cinder-block house, a blast of hot air rushed over me, as if it were being sucked into the room. The chirping of crickets roared from the tall grass surrounding my cool square of space. In the yard were a couple of tall coconut palms and a few small fruit trees that I hadn't noticed the night before when, in darkness, I arrived at my new home. Exhausted from the long drive south, I had hauled in one suitcase, thrown some sheets on the bed, and fallen asleep without really looking around.

Now I wanted to take it all in. I sat in a plastic chair out on the screened-in front porch. Sipping my coffee, I absorbed the smells and sounds of the South Florida environment.

The sun was big and bright, the air heavy and wet like a steam bath. Gentle breezes blew over me the aroma of boiling greenery, and I thanked God for electronic air. Only an occasional car passed on the narrow road that ran by the house. Ah, no traffic noise, I said to myself. This place will meet my meditative needs nicely. I was sure that my first pastorate would require lots of prayer time.

My eyes focused on a shiny silver mailbox bearing bold, black letters: REV. SIDNEY P. TRAINER. It was the first time I had seen "Rev." in front of my name. I was thrilled and frightened at the same time. A voice inside me said: It's right! Then another voice said: You have too many flaws —you're not pure of heart enough. The first voice responded: Shut up! It's right. The age-old conflict had been going on in me since I started thinking about divinity school and pastoring. "Well, I may not be perfect, but I won't let these people down," I said aloud.

I wasn't about to let anything spoil my first day as official pastor of the Fundamentalist Family of God Church. They had chosen me, so they must have seen something good. This little house wasn't just a house — it was the parsonage. My church was just down the street, and inside was the pastor's office — my office. Today was the beginning of a vocation and a life that I had been working toward for a long time.

A car rambled down the street and slowed to a stop out front. A man stuck his head out of the car window and looked around. It was Frank Eldridge, from the board of deacons. He saw my car and pulled up beside it.

I jumped up, ran into the house, and threw on a pair of jeans and a blouse. Stopping in front of the mirror, I ran a brush through my hair. There was a knock. I took a moment to calm myself, then walked to the door.

"Hi, Mr. Eldridge," I said, smiling as I opened the squeaky porch door. "Come in."

"Howdy, Reverend Trainer. I came to see if you had gotten here yet. I'm the welcoming committee," he said, chuckling. "And call me Frank."

Frank was a friendly, good-natured man. I had liked him immediately when I came for my interview with the deacons a few months earlier. He was like a bear, big and burly, and had a soft manner. Originally from Georgia, he still retained the remnants of a southern accent.

"I arrived late last night," I said as I motioned for him to sit. "Can I get you some coffee? I'm afraid that's all I can offer you at this point."

"Naw, nothing Pastor, thanks."

I sat down and waited for him to speak.

"So — how does it feel? The place okay?" he asked.

"It's just fine, Frank. Of course, I'll have to add some personal touches."

"Of course," he nodded. "If you need help with anything, just say the word."

As we sat making small talk, I suspected that Frank had something on his mind, that there was some agenda in this visit involving more than simply welcoming me.

The conversation lapsed, then Frank spelled it out. "Pastor, the deacons thought it would be helpful if I filled you in on a smidgen of church history. There's some, well, unfortunate matters that would be better heard from us than through the grapevine." He smiled and blushed a little. My curiosity was aroused and, for some reason, a red flag went up in my head.

"It's about the last two pastors we had," he went on. "You see, Reverend, our church has a tradition of using people from our own congregation or one of the other congregations in the denomination as our pastors. I guess you would call them 'lay pastors.' They usually don't have a formal education. They just feel the call. Some of them have a year of Bible school, at most. But the important thing to us was always that they felt the call real strong. We've always felt that the spirit would guide us in choosing the right person. The last couple of times, though, that didn't work real well. Maybe we weren't open enough to the spirit or something."

He paused and looked at me with a perplexed expression, as if he thought I could explain to him why the Holy Spirit had let them down. I said nothing.

"Anyway, the people we chose were not right for our church. Our last pastor, poor man, went crazy. He always was a little odd, Pastor Jim. But towards the end, his sermons and behavior got stranger and stranger. He was convinced that he was being chased by demons and started spending all his time on anti-demon activities. He put crosses and pictures of Jesus all over his office and at the parsonage here. His sermons became so downright hysterical on demon possession that you'da thought Satan himself was after him. He'd go on about how the congregation should be constantly vigilant and on the watch for demons waiting to jump into their souls. Finally, one Sunday he told the congregation to make animal sacrifices to God, then he went into detail about what to do with the blood. Well, after *that,* we had to ask him to step down as pastor. That musta been the final blow to him, because he became severely agitated and could be heard howling and raving from his home here, day and night."

Frank and I both turned our heads and looked into the living room and out the front door, as if we were checking to make sure that old Pastor Jim wasn't still there.

"The police finally came to take him to the state mental hospital. They'd put him in one of them straightjackets. Seems he'd been pulling his hair out in big chunks, and the police were afraid he'd hurt himself.

"When we came into the house afterwards, we got shook up good. He had painted the whole inside black. Everywhere on the black walls crosses were painted, probably with some poor little animal's blood. Seems he would lay prostrate for hours on the floor in front of one big cross of blood. The place was a mess of garbage and human excrement. Well, anyway—" Frank shook his head as if to knock out the memory, " —it was a bad time for us all. The congregation was real scared by the whole thing. I felt bad for the man, myself. He was just ... you know ... not right upstairs."

"What about the pastor before him?" I asked. I needed to change the subject, and hoped I wasn't going from bad to worse. Frank visibly brightened.

"Well, now, *he* was a real nice guy. Had a nice wife and two sweet children. Everybody loved Pastor Gary." Oh, good, I said to myself in relief. "That was the problem," Frank added suddenly.

"What do you mean?" I asked weakly.

"He was doing real well here. Seemed like he was the perfect pastor. Had charisma. Church attendance was at an all-time high." Frank seemed reluctant to go on.

"So what happened?" I asked, although I was beginning to get the picture.

"Missus Weston — she's one of our members — came home early from work one day with the flu. She walked in the house and found her daughter Melissa and our pastor together in the sack." Frank seemed compelled to explain. "I mean, she caught them having sexual intercourse. Yep, there was Melissa all tied up to the bed while Pastor Gary was humpin' away at her." Frank caught himself, as if suddenly realizing who he was talking to, and looked away. He was red right down to his fingertips.

He took a deep breath. "We didn't have to ask him to leave. He took off — and took Melissa with him. His wife and kids moved back to Ohio, too upset to stay here. Missus Weston still hasn't heard word one from Melissa. She's been real depressed around all that ever since." Frank leaned back in his chair and folded his hands in his lap, as if the dirty duty had been done.

We were silent for a few minutes. Then Frank came to the point.

"I guess besides letting you in on our ... uh ... difficult past, I'm also trying to explain why we chose you as pastor — I mean, besides the fact that you seem real nice and all. We decided that this time we should get someone who had the proper education for pastoring. At the congregational meeting we had, right after Pastor Gary left, the vote was unanimous: this time we'd do it right! Ain't no law says the person who feels the call can't be educated too. So, when we wrote the seminary in our pastoral search, and you answered, it seemed like our problems were over. This time we'd have a pastor who was educated and a woman! We're double-safe."

It struck me how they had stereotyped me as an educated woman of the cloth. I was immediately removed from the sexually wanton or even mentally ill realm of possibility. Women don't tie people to beds or become raving maniacs. And the education was like a little insurance policy. I had the Good Housekeeping Seal of Approval. The message the congregation was sending to me, through Frank, was that they fully expected me to be sane and sober. I guess that's not an unrealistic expectation of your pastor, I thought.

As Frank got into his car that day and drove away, I couldn't understand why I had such a tightening in my gut. Certainly, I'd be able to meet their expectations. I was going to be a stable, solid, spiritual leader. There were no loose ends here — were there?

II

Later that morning I drove around to orient myself to the area. I found the local convenience store and bought a few necessary groceries.

Loxihattchee was a small swamp town, with lots of marshes and a small lake. Most of the houses were one grade up from shack, and there were a number of trailers and trailer parks. The residents were from many different parts of the country. One thing the townspeople seemed to have in common was class — they ranged from poor to almost poor. It was hard to believe that the ocean, with its wealthy houses and expensive cars, was only about twenty miles east.

I noticed when I had come down to guest preach — my tryout, so to speak — that the congregation was an interesting mix. Most of the parishioners were white with various European combinations. There were also a few black families and a couple of Cuban families.

Race didn't appear to be an issue among these people. I guessed it was because so many of them had moved here fairly recently. There was even a transient population — snowbirds, they were called — that came down to Florida for six months during the fall and winter and then went back up north for the spring and summer. No one seemed to have an ownership attitude toward the place, which may have accounted for the lack of racial animosity. In the church, at least, the prevailing attitude was that everyone is equal in the eyes of the Lord.

This lack of ethnic consciousness was one of the reasons why I had taken the position of pastor here. I also liked that it was a small church — there were only about two hundred members. I didn't want to work in one of those huge churches with five pastors (pastor of education, pastor of visitation, pastor of music, etcetera). I wanted a nice intimate church, with people I could touch.

After I put away the groceries and gulped down a bowl of cereal, I took a nice cool bath and got ready for the best part of the day. I had promised myself that the afternoon of my first day would be a special gift to myself. I wanted to visit the church and spend some quiet meditative time taking in the spirit of the sanctuary, discerning what angels lived there and communing with the place that would be the focal point of my leadership.

It wasn't far, so I walked. By the time I reached the small building, I was dripping in the noon heat. I scanned the outside of the simple structure first, from the cross topping the wooden steeple, down the front to two large entrance doors. Then I climbed the few cement stairs and went in.

Immediately inside was a small foyer table on which there were stacks of flyers and religious literature. Large beams separated the foyer from the back of the sanctuary. I walked halfway down the center aisle and looked around me. It was cool and dark. Sunlight filtered in through a row of rectangular windows along the sides, slightly illuminating the sanctuary. More light came from small ceiling lamps above the altar.

A scent of damp wood mixed with the smell of grass fermenting outside. It was a sweet dank odor just this side of offensive. It's the smell of a swamp, I decided as I sat in a pew a few aisles back from the altar.

I squared myself in the seat, planted my feet flat on the floor, and took several deep breaths. When I felt centered, I closed my eyes and let my spirit search. Very soon I sensed a stillness in the place that was almost palpable. Outside I could hear sounds of birds chirping, locusts humming, and a distant train whistle; yet the silence inside the room was piercing. My senses were working at an optimum level, but nothing distracted my mind. My brain fell into this quietude like a rock down an empty well. The sensation would have been frightening if it weren't for an equally pervasive sense of peace. My heart rested, nerve endings relaxed. My body sank in repose, like a balloon slowly deflating.

After only a few moments I opened my eyes and was certain — the sanctuary was the home of the angels of stillness and serenity. My discovery was thrilling; this was a perfect place for worship and meditation. How lucky I am! I thought. But now that I know what's here, let me see what's going on in me.

I closed my eyes again and let myself drift. Almost instantly a face appeared from the recesses of my mind. It was the face of Jennifer Lee. The thought of her produced a tightening in my body which struggled against the angel of serenity. I finally let go and allowed the memory to surface.

III

Jennifer Lee had been a professor of mine in seminary. The first course I had taken with her was Feminist Theology.

It was the spring semester of my second year, and as each day passed I became more and more enamored of her. She had an easy, relaxed style of teaching. When she lectured, she'd sit on the edge of a desk and occasionally walk around the room, as if she were speaking to each student individually. I could still smell the perfume she wore, which left a trace of her behind as she passed by.

In the classroom one could approach her easily — any question could be asked, any subject broached. On a one-to-one basis, however, she was strangely standoffish; she became stiff and cool. I was confused by this behavior. But as time went on this air of hers only aided in making her persona altogether intriguing to me.

By the time the semester was coming to a close, I had managed to make her notice me. She didn't seem to mind the extra little discussions we had after class or my walking her to her car; her wall appeared to be coming down.

One day during the last week of the semester, as we lingered in the parking lot discussing Biblical symbolism, she suddenly looked at me squarely and said, "You know, I'm writing a paper for publication, hopefully, on Christian ethics and euthanasia."

"Sounds like pretty heavy stuff," I said.

"Yeah," she laughed. "But I need someone to type it up for me. My typing's a sin. Would you be interested in doing that? I'll pay you, of course."

"Sure!" I said, a little too quickly.

"As a matter of fact," she added, pausing for a moment, "how does spending a couple of weeks on the Cape this summer sound to you?"

"The Cape?" Excitement rose inside me.

"Yes. You see, that's when I'll be writing most of the paper and it would really be nice if I could get it typed as I'm writing it. But only, of course, if that works out for you."

I couldn't respond right away; my brain and mouth didn't seem to be connected at that moment. She scanned me intensely.

"Well, why don't you think about it for a couple of days, see if it works out with your schedule." She had deftly shifted the mood to a more casual one. As she opened her car door and slid into the driver's seat I felt the air returning to my lungs. I bent down and looked at her through the car window.

"Can you let me know by, say, Thursday?" she asked.

"I can let you know now," I answered. "That sounds really terrific, and I'm free for several weeks after the semester."

"Great!" she exclaimed. "Let's talk about it some more tomorrow after class."

"Okay, see you then."

I backed away and watched her drive off. I think I could learn a lot from her, I pondered as I walked toward the dorm.

I found myself having a hard time controlling my excitement. I didn't understand why I was so taken with Jennifer. I'd had crushes on teachers before, but I had assumed that I'd outgrown such things. I decided that it must have something to do with my being so involved school. Boy, I really do love studying theology, I marveled.

IV

Jennifer had a pretty little cottage situated on a marshy inlet in Wellfleet. It was secluded and quiet, and the beach was just down the road. The day I arrived, I was admiring the wildflowers around the house when she answered the door.

"Hi, Sidney. Welcome," she greeted warmly. She gave me a quick hug and insisted on carrying my suitcase inside.

As she showed me around the house and grounds, I could hardly take my eyes off her. She wore an oversized flannel shirt that hung open just enough to expose the tops of her full breasts. She had had her hair cut short and straight, and her bangs were brushed to the side, off her forehead. The brown color had a golden shine to it. Her face was relaxed, and when she smiled, her hazel eyes sparkled. Age lines were beginning to crease her skin. Her top lip was slightly uneven, giving it a quality that made one want to look at it a lot. Her body was small and evenly proportioned.

Of course, I had noticed many of her physical aspects before; but for some reason, in this setting she seemed to be a different person. As she pointed out some of the finer aspects of her little spot on the earth, it was nearly impossible for me to tear my eyes away from her in order to look at anything else.

At dinner that evening Jennifer was talkative, and nervous. As we drank our after-dinner coffee, it occurred to me that she had probably noticed me looking at her. I became instantly embarrassed at the idea and scolded myself for gawking, after which I purposefully tried not to look at her.

By the end of the second day we had established a little routine of meals, work, beach time, and quiet time.

We ended our days by reading in the living room. I found it difficult, however, to concentrate on my book during these evenings. Periodically I would get up, walk out onto the porch, and stare into the night. Sometimes when I moved around the cottage I was aware of Jennifer looking at me. I imagined that she might be concerned about whether I was having a good time or not.

The truth was that I was having a great time — great and tortured, that is. I had known as soon as I found myself in this salty little haven that I had fallen madly in love with Jennifer. Never before had I experienced feelings this strong for anyone. The fact that we were both women and that the feelings were definitely sexual drove me wild with conflict. But as disconcerting as it all was, I knew that the desire was stronger than the conflict. As traumatized as I was by the thought that something might happen, I was more deeply pained by the possibility that something might not.

As the days passed, I lived half in reality and half in fantasy. All I could think about was her naked body. When I tried to pray, I couldn't; I was quite sure that God didn't approve of these feelings — it was a foregone conclusion that God didn't dig homosexuality. Although up until then I hadn't needed to research the issue in the Bible, I'd heard often enough that it was condemned as sin.

How easy it was for me to push my spiritual life aside for passion, I thought. I was somewhat ashamed of myself. But my wanting her was so powerful that it almost made itself right, just by the strength of it. I found myself trying to make a deal with God: if God would allow me just this one time, I would never succumb again.

V

It was clear and sunny in the afternoon of my twelfth day on the Cape. We had taken a swim and were lying on a blanket. While we baked in the sun, I was fantasizing about Jennifer's breasts. I loved these times on the beach, when I could see so much of her body.

My daydream was interrupted by questions which had been plaguing my mind these past two weeks: How did she feel? Could this desire I have possibly be just mine? It seemed to me that the sheer power of it would cause it to spill over to her. But maybe that was wishful thinking on my part.

Almost as if Jennifer heard my thoughts, she suddenly said, "There's a certain romance about this place, isn't there?"

"Uh-huh, yeah," I responded, hoping she would say more.

"Maybe it's just that it's so quiet and low-key, but I always find that my mind drifts off when I'm here. I dream more at night too."

I couldn't resist: "What kind of dreams?"

"Oh ... some of them are sexual, if you must know," she said with a laugh. She turned so that she was facing me, up on her elbow with her head resting in her hand. Her expression was mischievous, her mouth curled up in a half smile. I looked over at her and couldn't help but laugh.

"I'm waiting," she said.

"Okay, okay, what are the details?"

"None of your business!" She shifted, still smiling, to lie on her back.

"Oh, that's not fair," I whined, as I sat up.

"Okay," she said, "you tell me about one of your sexual fantasies and I'll tell you about a dream. Deal?"

I didn't respond for a minute. I gazed at her tanned body lying there, hardly covered by her skimpy bathing suit. Finally I said, quietly, "I'm not sure you'd want to hear about my fantasies."

I couldn't tell whether she had gotten the picture or not, but she started to squirm under my gaze. A few minutes went by in awkward silence. Then she said, "I think I'm getting too much sun. I'm going back to the house to take a shower." Within seconds she had jumped up and was gone.

I sat there, confused. Then a revelation pushed itself through the muddle. She wants me to follow her! Immediately convinced of the truth of this, I sat, unable to move. It felt as if I were attached to that small bit of beach like a sand statue.

Finally, with some effort I pried myself loose and began walking slowly toward the house. With each step my anticipation and excitement grew more staggering, so that by the time I reached the cottage I couldn't see straight. It seemed as if my consciousness had been short-circuited — that neurons were firing off in my head like it was the Fourth of July.

I opened the screen door. It squeaked loudly, annoyingly announcing my arrival. As I walked toward my room I saw Jennifer standing in the bathroom, wrapped in a towel. Uncertain about what I should do, I scurried into my room.

"Sid," she called out to me. "You can take a shower if you want to. I'm finished in here now!"

"Okay, thanks," I yelled back.

I hung my beach towel on the back of a chair and slipped out of my bathing suit. Checking to see that Jennifer was out of the bathroom, I quickly walked into it. I turned on the shower and stepped under it. As I was lathering up my hair and body, a profound disappointment set in. I decided that my idea about her wanting me to follow her had been just my imagination. She probably doesn't have feelings like I have at all, I thought.

I finished showering and began drying off in front of the large mirrored medicine cabinet. I grabbed my hairbrush and felt my heart brim over with self-pity. When I tried to brush through a knot that was being particularly difficult, I couldn't take the frustration. I threw the brush on the floor in anger. Then, with a sigh, I bent down and picked it up. I was holding the brush in my hand, staring at it blankly, when I heard a knock at the bathroom door. I jumped.

"Sid, do you mind if I come in to get something?"

"Oh, sure," I said as nonchalantly as I could, while wrapping a towel around me. "Come on in."

Jennifer came in and stood next to me as she opened the medicine cabinet. She took something out and slid the door closed. We stood side by side in the mirror. She was still wearing her towel. I had begun to brush my hair again slowly when I noticed that Jennifer was just standing there staring at my reflection. I stopped my activity and looked back at her.

The moment our eyes met in the mirror, I knew that my former intuition about her had been right. She reached over and tugged at my towel until it came loose and fell to the floor. Then she let hers drop. Our eyes inspected each other's naked reflections. Her breasts were ample, the fleshy part drooping down, resting on her chest. They looked very white against her tanned skin. Her brown nipples were large and luscious. Her belly was firm with a slight bulge above her fluffy brown pubic hair. Her thighs were shapely but not overly fond of exercise.

I raised my hand and ran it lightly down her front. The tips of her nipples immediately formed into hard points. She sighed at my touch. Then she took my hand, brought it to her mouth, and began kissing my palm.

My legs twitched with excitement as I moved to embrace her. Our bodies met softly. She smelled of sea and shampoo. The image of her breasts lingered in my mind. I pulled back a little and began to kiss her neck, shoulders, and chest, then moved down to her hardened nipples. I lifted the heavy round flesh of her bosom, cupping it in my hands as I licked and sucked the wondrous brown tips.

Jennifer grabbed onto the sink to steady herself and murmured, "Oh, Sid. I want you so much." She lifted my face to hers and we kissed. Her lips tasted fresh and sweet. Her tongue pushed its way into my mouth and I sucked it in. Tickling, stinging sensations spread from my lips to the back of my neck. Goose bumps popped up all over me, my body began to throb, and my crotch ached. We parted and looked into each other's eyes. Hers were gleaming. I moved to take her mouth again, but she stopped me, took my hand, and led me to her bedroom.

The sun was just setting, and an orange glow lit the room. Clean, crisp ocean air blew through the open windows. The curtains rose with each puff of wind, then sank back against the sill, as if the room were breathing. Her bed was of old brass. It creaked loudly as we climbed on it. We lay facing each other, absorbed in each other's nakedness. I began caressing her in all those places I had dreamt about — the forbidden, hidden parts that were reserved for one's lover. Her skin rose in tiny bumps under my fingers. My hands shook in excitement.

Our lips joined again. We played our tongues in and around each other's mouths. The feel and taste of her mouth, along with the sensation of groping hands, set me on fire. I wanted to fill her. I pushed her shoulders down on the bed and moved on top of her, licking her eyes, ears, and neck. Then I fondled her breasts, squeezing and releasing them. I sucked at her hard nipples as my hands forced them to pop up for my mouth's grasp. Noises came from my gut as my body slithered over hers. She moaned, her body twisting and grinding, responding to mine. She pressed her pelvis into me, grabbed my buttocks, and pulled my cunt against hers.

When she relaxed her hold on me, I pulled free and quickly glided down, diving my face into her wet mound. Slowly, softly I licked her. She shivered and yelped. Her hole, deep and dark, bubbled in its juices. I spread her legs wide with my arms, and thrusting with my tongue, I plunged into her again and again.

She cried out, "Oh, Sidney, please, oh please." I jammed my tongue more deeply into her, wiggling it around as she sucked me in. Desire raged through me — the desire to be completely inside her, swallowed up by her. As I stabbed her with my tongue, I fantasized that I was ramming my whole body deeper and deeper into her. With each thrust, my face knocked up against her rock-hard clitoris. Lost in my own illusion, I imagined my body as a giant, pulsating presence driving further and deeper, desperately striving to reach an imaginary incandescent place inside her.

She screamed cries of mounting delight. Suddenly her legs flailed wildly, her belly twitched, and her cavern opened wide. Then, with a fierce clenching she closed in on me, holding me tightly in her clutch. Her buttocks and thighs were locked in spasm as she pleaded, "Please, Sid, no more, no more ... oh ... oh ... oh ... God." Cum flowed out of her and her body loosened again, her vagina fluttering as her second orgasm played itself out.

I couldn't stop. I was out of control, driven to reach that imaginary place where my throbbing body would lie. With a massive blast of effort I plunged frantically, until at last splendorous waves of light and heat enveloped me. Orgasm surged and flowed over and over me. I convulsed and gyrated until my strength was drained and my flesh went limp. I was floating in warm, white space.

After a while Jennifer pulled me up gently and held me. Her breathing was heavy as she wrapped herself tightly around my sagging body.

VI

I snapped out of my trance. As my eyes came back into focus I gazed at the sleek wooden cross that hung on the back wall of the altar, and the podium from which I would be preaching. "Oh, God," I pleaded, as a cloud of despair fell over me. I came here, I said to myself, to begin my vocation as a servant of God. I should be thinking about my work, my congregation, my church. And what do I do? I sink into oblivion about *her.*

I hung my head and covered my face with my hands, trying to hide from the world. Tears flowed out from underneath my hands and squeezed slowly from between my fingers, falling to the floor.

I had wanted, so badly, to escape from Jennifer. One of my reasons for taking this parish was because it was so far away from her. I had hoped to be able to forget the past and turn my attention to my work and my spiritual life. But she was still with me, as if I had packed her in my suitcase.

How am I going to stop thinking about her and go on with my life? I asked myself. Or, what if — a painful possibility emerged in my mind — what if I fall in love with another woman! "No!" I yelled out with conviction. Then to myself: That's the end of it! Neither I nor this church can afford to become involved in any scandals. God help me, I won't fall back into that place of sin that held me so completely for one solid summer. I will pray day and night if necessary to rid myself of thoughts of her, or *any* sexual desires.

When I raised my head and removed my hands from my face — now free of tears — I saw a woman standing silently by the organ to the left of the pulpit. She looked like a vision; I thought momentarily in my deranged mental state, that she might be an angel come to comfort me. Her wispy hair was white-blonde, and she wore a flowered housedress over a full figure. As she took a few steps toward me, I noticed a waddle in her walk. When she reached the pew where I was sitting, her face came into view. She had small, green eyes and her skin was a smooth, flawless, creamy white. She spoke: "Um ... I didn't mean to disturb you. You're the new pastor — I remember you from when you came to preach. I just came in here to make sure everything was set up for tomorrow's service. Oh — I'm Winifred Swenson, the church secretary — *your* secretary now. I'll leave you alone." She turned to exit.

"No, wait!" I called to her. "I was meditating," I explained, "but I'm finished now. It's nice to meet you, Winifred." I stood up and extended my hand.

She grabbed it and smiled. "Call me Win!" I noted the firmness of her handshake. So maybe she wasn't an angel, but she had a nice aura; I could sense that immediately.

"Would you like to see your office, Pastor?" she asked. "Maybe you'd like to get settled in."

"Yeah, that would be great," I replied. "I should start working on my sermon for tomorrow pretty soon."

She led the way. I noted again her little waddle; it might have been funny, except that I found it somehow endearing. Win showed me into a spacious office with a large modern desk, a number of metal folding chairs, and two stuffed chairs. The room was clean and void of clutter. There was a large bookcase, which was mostly empty, and several windows along the back wall.

"I'm so glad it has windows," I said to Win.

She smiled and nodded. "You'll be doing your counseling in here so I have a separate office through there." She pointed to a door in the middle of the wall, and we walked over and looked in at her workspace.

I hardly knew this woman but I felt comfortable enough to honestly say to her, "I'm so glad you're close by."

"Oh, I'm your right-hand man, all right, Pastor," she said, with a twinkle in her eyes.

"You know, I think I'm going to enjoy working with you," I said enthusiastically.

Win let out a hoot. "Pastor, I think we're going to have a ball!" We both laughed. She had, within a few minutes, accomplished a significant lifting of my spirits. Maybe she *is* an angel, I thought. "Well, I'm going to take off now. Give you some time to write that sermon."

"Thanks, Win. I'll see you tomorrow."

"The Good Lord willing," she shot back as she walked out the door.

VII

My alb was a white tailored robelike garment. The collar was round with a V-shaped slit down the front. Around my neck I wore a large silver chain that carried a plain silver cross. The sleeves of the alb were long with wide cuffs. Wearing it gave me a strange, regal-like feeling, but I liked the meaning the vestment gave me. It was the uniform identifying me as clergy.

I sat in a large oak chair up on the altar and looked out at the congregation. The parishioners' faces were serious. A thrill went through me as I scanned my flock. These were my people. I was their spiritual leader — their comforter in difficult times, their counselor and confessor. I couldn't help but love them even though they were still strangers to me.

We stood for the opening hymn. The organist played a short intro and we began to sing. I held my head high, my hymnal solid in my hands, and belted out the familiar tune. I loved singing hymns; and today it was particularly enjoyable, singing praises to God with my new congregation.

We were into the third verse when I happened to look over at the organist. My heart skipped a beat — it was as if someone had struck a match in a blackened room. Her alluring beauty pierced my consciousness, and I forgot to sing. It may have come from the joy of the music or from something I knew nothing about, but she seemed to glow. I remembered to sing, and I turned away but found myself within moments drawn back to her. She had black wavy shoulder-length hair. In a heart-shaped face with prominent cheekbones, her eyes were blue and enormous. Even though she was sitting, I could tell that she was small-statured.

We finished the hymn with a loud *"A-men"* and sat down. I looked around the sanctuary and searched the faces of the congregation. No one seemed to have noticed my indiscreet staring at the organist. I dared to glance over at her again. She looked up toward me and our eyes met. A big smile broke out on her face, lighting up her already glowing persona even more. I half smiled back and quickly looked away, flushed with embarrassment.

A deacon read the Old Testament selection from the Bible. When he finished, he took his seat. I stood up, walked to the podium, and laid open my notes and Bible on the stand. I took a deep breath and looked out at the people. I spoke slowly, deliberately, and with the confidence of one who knows what she wants to say.

I read from the New Testament: "If a son shall ask bread of any of you that is a father, will he give him a stone? Or if he ask a fish, will he for a fish give him a serpent? Or if he ask an egg, will he offer him a scorpion? If ye, then, being evil, know how to give good gifts unto your children, how much more shall your heavenly Father give unto you to them that ask Him?"

I stepped around the podium, out into full view of the congregation. "Will you pray with me, please?" I closed my eyes and raised my arms up and out to the sides, with the palms of my hands turned up. "May the words of my mouth and the meditation of our hearts be acceptable in Thy sight, oh God, our Rock and our Redeemer." I went back to the podium and preached my first sermon as the Reverend Sidney Trainer to my first congregation, the Fundamentalist Family of God.

At the end of the sermon, I left them with a charge. I stepped down from the altar, stood in the front of the first row of pews, and tried to make eye contact with each person as the words came through me: "I challenge every one of you today to let the love of God into your life, to own for yourself what God freely gives, to open yourself to the light and power that is yours. Know that you are loved — not because of what you do, but because of who you are. And who are you? You are God's child. As you go through this week, turn off your mind when it starts to tell you that you don't deserve God's love. Open your heart! Be assured as you live your life, from the small daily tasks to the large heavy burdens, that God is with you. God is with you in everything — simply, because *you* are a child of God."

When I finished, the sanctuary was absolutely still. As I turned and went back to my chair I thought I could hear the dust settle. Finally the organ began to play softly, and as we sang the closing hymn I could see a gleam in the eyes of the people.

VIII

Later, during coffee hour in the rec room, Win introduced me around to some of the parishioners. John Samuels, the church custodian, was filling me in on the strengths and weaknesses of the church building when Win grabbed my arm. "Excuse us a minute, John, I have to introduce Pastor Sidney to our music director."

My legs were weak as Win dragged me over to the coffee table where Joanne Mataresse, the goddess of the church organ, stood. Taller than I had guessed, she carried a healthy amount of shapely flesh on maybe a five-foot-five frame, and wore snug-fitting jeans and a t-shirt.

"Joanne," Win called to her as we approached, "let me formally introduce you to Reverend Sidney Trainer." Joanne turned and put her cup down. Smiling, she took my hand in both of hers and gave it a firm shake.

"It's so wonderful to have you here, Pastor! We've all been looking forward to your coming — especially me." The room was getting extremely hot. Sweat began to form on my upper lip.

"It's real nice to meet you too, Joanne. I enjoyed your playing so much today. We're lucky to have a good organist."

"She's a fine choir director too," Win piped in.

"Well, adequate I guess," Joanne said modestly. "The best thing about being choir director is that you get to wear anything you want under the choir robe." She smiled and pointed to her jeans.

"Yeah, well, same goes when you wear an alb," I said. I lifted my alb to expose my shabby cutoffs. The three of us cackled in glee. Joanne seemed particularly tickled, squeezing my arm as she giggled. When the laughter subsided, Win had turned away from us and was talking to someone else, leaving me and Joanne standing together alone in awkward silence.

Joanne broke the ice. "It'll be a relief to have someone who knows what they're doing at the liturgy meetings."

It suddenly dawned on me that we'd be seeing each other quite often. "Oh, that's right. What night do we meet?" As we talked, I was becoming more aware of my attraction to this woman. I screamed at myself inside: Stop it!

"Thursdays," she answered. "We have them at my place. You should come for dinner this Thursday."

"Thanks, that really would be nice, but I can't this week. Maybe some other time."

"Sure, we've got lots of time," she said, undaunted. "I don't know what I was thinking. You probably have a lot of unpacking to do this week."

"That's true," I acknowledged. I thought: No way am I going to be alone with you. I have to be real careful here. I know myself all too well. I can't and won't let anything happen!

Win returned, and I said, "Well, I think I should meet a few more people. Don't you, Win?"

Win looked puzzled. "Okay, but almost everyone's left by now."

Joanne smiled her wonderful smile. "I've got to run too. See you Thursday night, Pastor Trainer."

"Right. I'm looking forward to it."

"Bye, Win." Joanne waved and was gone.

Win looked at me with a funny expression on her face. "What?" I asked.

"You look pale as a ghost! Are you okay?" She put a motherly hand on my forehead. "I think you might be coming down with that flu that's been going around here — one of those nasty summer bugs."

"No, I'm fine Win, really. It's just been a very big day, you know?"

Unconvinced, she continued to study me. "Maybe, but you feel so hot. You call me if you start getting sick," she ordered.

"Sure, but I'm fine — really."

We left the rec room and headed toward our offices. I was dying to know more about Joanne, even though I knew that I shouldn't be. I gave in. "Is Joanne married?" I asked casually.

"No," Win answered. "Funny thing, isn't it? She's so pretty. No kids either, that I know of. I think she has a fella, though. She's mentioned a man a couple of times. But she's never brought him to church."

"Oh," I said. I couldn't help being markedly disappointed. But at the same time I was angry with myself for feeling that way. "She's probably engaged or about to be," I added, still fishing.

"Probably," Win answered, nodding.

That takes care of that! I said to myself with relief. "Thank you, Jesus," I muttered softly.

IX

The first weeks passed quickly as I settled in nicely to a routine of meetings, counseling sessions, and Sundays. I was enjoying my work immensely. My spiritual life was vibrant and growing. I felt God's presence clearly when I sought guidance in all that I did. I came to sincerely love the people in the church. Many of them truly wanted to have God in their lives in a very real way.

And God never failed me, providing me with the words and wisdom I needed in every situation. A spirituality was alive among us all, and the people were less preoccupied with the harsh dogmas for which the denomination was so famous. Together we were learning to rely on God's love, teaching ourselves to stop and listen for His direction and to act in ways that love requires. Day by day we were learning together about Christ's only law to love God and each other.

Each day, I meditated in the sanctuary when no one was around. There, the angels of stillness and serenity nurtured me. I did a lot of praying about my lust for Joanne. Twice a week I saw her, and even though I kept a certain amount of distance between us, I was being more and more drawn to her, both physically and as a potential friend. She was energetic and fun-loving, talented and intelligent. All in all, there was nothing I didn't love about her.

I couldn't understand why God wouldn't take away my desire for her body. I considered the idea that it may be a test, but I didn't really believe that God tested us in that way. Anyway, my faith was not in question here; I felt just as close to God when I had lustful feelings as I did when I had no conscious sexual thoughts. In fact, that's probably what confused me the most. How could I have such sinful thoughts and yet still be so close to God? I wished I understood why God was allowing this.

One Sunday night, after working late in my office, I exited the building by the back door and walked around to the front, where John Samuels always kept the outside lights on after dark. When I turned the corner, I saw someone sitting on the front steps. As I drew closer I recognized Joanne. I approached her cautiously.

"Joanne, is that you?" I asked, quietly.

"Oh, Sidney. Yeah, it's me. I didn't realize you were still here."

"I was working in my office," I explained. "Are you all right?" She looked as if she'd been crying; her eyes were red and puffy. When she didn't respond right away, I sat down next to her.

After a minute she spoke. "To tell you the truth, Sid, I don't really know what's wrong. I guess I'm just lonely. You see, I've been seeing this guy for about a year now. He's the latest in a series of men I've dated. I thought that things would be different with him, that he might be ... uh ... the one, you know?" I nodded. "Well, like I said, it's been about a year and I just don't feel like it's right. It's the same as with all the others. I start getting ... I don't know, bored, I guess. And I don't want him to touch me ... you know, sexually?" I nodded again. "To tell you the truth, I enjoy the time I spend here at the church much more than being with him."

When she stopped talking I became nervous, and for some reason I felt a need to make light of her last comment. "It is fun here. The people are warm and enjoy a good time. I can see why you like it." I was getting restless. "Walk me to my house and I'll get us some iced tea."

She looked at me squarely, then stood up. "Okay, that sounds good."

We walked toward the parsonage in silence. There was a bright ring of haze around the moon, softly lighting our way. The night was sultry, with just the hint of a breeze that, instead of cooling me off, only reminded me of how hot I was. As we sauntered down the road, the chemistry between us changed. This was the first time that Joanne had told me anything personal about herself; the closeness that I had been avoiding was inadvertently finding its way to us.

"Have a seat," I said, pointing to a chair on the porch. I'll get us some drinks. Iced tea okay?"

"Okay, unless you have something stronger?"

I laughed. "Who, me?"

"Yeah," she smiled, "I didn't think so."

I went in and poured our drinks. I watched Joanne through the front door; her mood had brightened. We sat sipping our tea. I waited for her to continue telling me what was going on with her. Our chairs were close together, and the hair on my arm next to hers bristled. Her nearness was making my insides churn. I caught myself lapsing into mental images of kissing and touching her. She had opened our friendship up to a greater depth this night, and that made my desire for her reach a new pitch.

"Sidney," she began, "it's so nice to have you for a friend. I don't have a lot of friends, especially anyone close to my own age. You're very special to me." She paused and I shook with anxiety. "It feels good just being around you." My heart was pounding in my ears. What would she think if she knew what I was feeling? I wondered. "You know, we should do more together — don't you think?" She didn't wait for me to answer. "I'm going to have more free time as soon as I end this thing with Jack — he's the guy I was telling you about — I don't see the point in going on with him. I'm having more fun sitting here on the porch with you than I've ever had with him."

I froze in my seat. Silently I prayed: Help! Then I took a deep breath and tried to relax. "Your friendship means a lot to me too, Joanne," I began. "I spend a lot of time with people, but I'm always in my public role. It's hard for me to have real give and take with the people in the church. I feel like I can talk to you pretty freely, though. I'm glad for both of us that we had this chance to talk."

I looked over at her and my blood began to boil. Her big eyes, saddened and red earlier, were clear and bright again, and she was radiating that glow. I felt a wetness seep out of me and squirmed in my seat. An irrational notion flashed through my mind that somehow, she knew my body craved hers.

Joanne finished her iced tea and stood up. "It's getting late, I'd better go." I got up too and faced her; I was almost a head taller. Suddenly she flung her arms around me. I responded stiffly. "Thanks so much for being there for me tonight, Sid."

"My pleasure," I mumbled. I was afraid that in another moment I'd sink right into her. I gently pulled myself away. "I'll walk you to your car," I croaked.

"Oh no, I'll be fine. You must be exhausted. I'll see you this week, right?"

"Right!" I managed a smile.

Then she was gone. I watched her melt into the darkness and fell back into my chair. As I sank into a physical and emotional heaviness, a dark sadness flooded my soul.

X

In the following weeks, I made sure that I was never alone with Joanne. Whenever she tried making plans with me, I found some excuse. As much as I didn't like hurting her feelings, I feared my own more.

My desire for her was unceasing. The only way I got any relief was to become completely engrossed in my work. I hoped that in time my lust would die.

I thought I was handling things quite well, though the constant balancing act was draining, the fight to cut her out of my life took a lot of energy. I experienced more and more that strength-sapping emptiness I had felt that night on the porch. With all my might, I prayed and suffered and held on to my integrity. The strain of all that emotional holding back eventually lowered my overall vitality. I knew I no longer had the clarity and energy that I had so easily and naturally brought to the pulpit in the first few weeks.

Then, one Sunday during the service, something unexpected happened. I had been practicing my latest ritual of not looking over at the organ so that I could get through the service without having to see Joanne. The music stopped, and the deacon began reading the text that came before the sermon. Instead of sitting in her usual place near the organ, Joanne walked out into my line of vision and sat down in the center of the church next to a dark, curly-haired man I had never seen before. When she slid in next to him, they smiled at each other and she wrapped her arm warmly around his.

Oh my God, she's found ... the *one,* a voice gasped inside of me. My heart sank, and my hands and legs felt like rubber as I got up to preach. I tightened my hold on the podium and, as if on automatic pilot, I delivered an emotionless sermon. From that moment on, the whole service was a blur.

My mind didn't work well all that day. Somehow, I managed to drag myself through the evening service. Joanne and her boyfriend didn't show up that night, which made things a little easier. Later, I lay in bed trying to talk myself out of the rotten place I was in. "It's for the best, you know that. You can't have her anyway. It's over now. Let it rest." But the pain was not the kind that could be reasoned away.

The next day, I went to the church office to counsel a parishioner. I still carried the tightening in my stomach from the day before. It was unrelenting, constant; but I had begun to accept that I would probably be feeling the pain for a while.

Mickey was an old, shriveled up, sweetheart of a man. Everyone called him Old Mick. I was curious about what was on his mind. He was right on time for his appointment. Settling himself into a chair across from me, he began talking immediately. He seemed nervous.

"Pastor, I have to say I feel a little funny coming to you like this. You're just a kid — no offense! But I thought about it and, well, you do have a sort of maturity beyond your years, I think. Anyway, you are the pastor, and I need to get something off my chest that's been bothering me for some time. I sure couldn't talk to those last two poor excuses ... uh ... well ... no mind. Anyway, it's like this. I have trouble with people." He curled his lip over his teeth and stared out the window behind me.

"But Mick," I said, confused, "you get along so well with everyone. There's not a soul in this church that doesn't think you're a pretty terrific guy."

"I know, I know." Now he looked straight at me. "But I don't like people." Seeing my perplexed expression, he went on. "You see, it's like this. When I went to that movie about the big shark — *Jaws* — I felt sorry for the shark when they got him at the end."

"Well, Mick," I said, "so you love animals. There's no sin in that. In fact, I think all of God's creatures deserve the same love and respect from us that God has for them. We don't pay enough attention to our environment in general, if you ask me —"

Mick stopped me cold and held up his hand. "But I enjoyed it when the shark ate up the people." His eyes grew intensely serious as he slammed the point home. "It's not my love of animals that bothers me, Pastor, it's my hatred of people. People as a group, that is — there are a few individuals I don't hate," he finished.

"Hmm," I mumbled. "Hmm." I met his gaze but didn't know quite what to say. "I think ... umm, maybe we need to talk about this some more, Mick. Can you come in, say, on a regular basis for a while? Maybe we can get to the bottom of what's going on."

"Uh-huh," Mick nodded, looking relieved. "That sounds right. I had a feeling it wasn't a problem that could be solved in one day."

"I'm really glad you came in today, though," I reassured him. "Getting it out in the open is a start in the right direction. And I'm really pleased that you can be so honest. Talk to Win about making an appointment for next week."

He smiled and rose slowly. "Thanks, Pastor. I do feel a little better now that I've told someone." He walked through to Win's office. I felt guilty for not giving him more time, but I just couldn't handle anything that heavy — not today.

I heard Old Mick leave Win's office. He had left the connecting door open. I leaned back in my chair and closed my eyes. A picture of Joanne and that man sitting together so affectionately flashed across my mind. The familiar heaviness came upon me, and I breathed a long sigh. Soon I heard a vaguely familiar voice coming from Win's office. The person was speaking in an almost monotone pitch, and I noted a deadness in the sound. I sat up sharply. The voice was mine! I went in to investigate. Win was studying a small tape recorder on her desk. She looked up at me.

"Hi, Sid. Want to listen to your sermon from yesterday's morning service?"

"It sounds awful!" I whined.

"It's not awful. It was a good sermon. People never like the sound of their own voices on tape," she said, matter-of-factly.

"Did I really drone on like that?" I was horrified.

"You were fine," Win assured me. "But, since you brought it up, I have noticed that you seem a little preoccupied or depressed lately. Is something wrong?"

Oh great, I thought, everyone has probably noticed. Little Miss Radar Brain read my mind. "I doubt anyone else has noticed. I'm closer to you than most, you know. I see the little changes." I didn't say anything right away, wondering if I could trust this kind, wise woman with the truth. I decided to keep it vague.

"Yeah, I've been dealing with a personal problem lately, and I've got an internal struggle going on. It's so hard to know what's right any more."

"What's right about what?" Win asked in her direct way. I felt her eyes studying me.

"What's right in the eyes of God," I answered.

"Why don't you ask God?"

"I have, Win, over and over."

"And?"

"And nothing."

"Hmm," Win was thinking. "Perhaps if you talked to a person, you could get some direction from her," she smiled. I appreciated her willingness to help, but couldn't bring myself to tell her.

"Not yet, Win. I'm still trying to work this out on my own."

"Okay," she said. Now she was looking at me tenderly, like someone who cares enough not to push.

"I think I'll go for a walk. I'm a little restless," I announced. Win nodded, and I left the church by the back door and ambled around to the front. I crossed the street to take in the full view of the building.

While standing there, I looked to the west and saw that although it was sunny where I stood, a gray-black wall was approaching. I could feel the air pressure around me changing quickly. Fantastic, I said to myself, a rainstorm's heading for us. I loved the way the rains came in Florida. You could actually see the sheet of drops coming at you. I would often stand and let the dark blanket glide over me and, in time, pass. As it continued its journey, I would stand soaked and watch the sun return. Afterwards, I'd sometimes see two or three rainbows.

I stood facing the storm as it rapidly came closer. It seemed to be only a couple of yards away when I heard a car come up the street behind me. I turned to look as it pulled up in front of the church. It was Joanne! In the driver's seat was the man I had seen her with at church. As the rain overtook me, I saw her give him a quick kiss and get out of the car.

Something grabbed my chest and squeezed the air out. My brain screamed: Not in my face — don't do this to me! I had to move, had to get away from her. As I turned back toward the storm, large wet balls of rain slapped at me. Rain-battered, I moved swiftly, bending my head against the assault and wishing I could just hit the ground and explode like the water drops.

Then I heard her. "Sidney, wait."

"No, leave me alone!" I shouted.

"But Sidney, please, I want to talk."

"I don't want to know about it," I said under my breath. I walked faster, hoping to lose her.

"Sidney." Her voice was closer; she had come into my storm.

I started running, barely able to see where I was going as globs of water pelted my eyes. After a while I knew I wasn't on the road any more. My breathing was heavy and my feet began to drag. Still I ran, knowing I couldn't face her.

I was near exhaustion when I suddenly tripped and flew, spread-eagle, into a warm mud puddle. I tried to get up, but my feet kept slipping out from under me. I gave up the fight and rolled over onto my back. As the rainwater washed the dirt off my eyes, I saw a woman towering over me. It was Joanne. She knelt down and pushed her drenched hair out of her face.

"Sidney, what's wrong?" she shouted. "Are you hurt?" She looked anguished.

I just lay there looking up at her beautiful, dripping countenance as the last shred of control, that I had so masterfully held in my grip, slipped away. It went like a whale crashing through the sea. My hands clutched at its slimy back trying uselessly to hold on until it kicked itself free, leaving me to sink in its shadow. Slowly I sat up, and she moved closer. Quietly and firmly I said, "This is what's wrong." I grabbed her arms tightly, pulled her toward me, and kissed her hard.

Gripping her hair, I forced her mouth open. I jammed my tongue inside and massaged hers, as it lay trapped and helpless. My head whirled and my body came alive.

I relaxed my hold on her. Instead of pulling away, she offered herself to me. I ran my fingers down her back and around to her front, sliding them up under her blouse. As I stroked her breasts through her wet bra, my blood sizzled. I unsnapped the bra and grasped her flesh. My passion, so long pent up, was bursting in my groin, shooting down my legs to my toes. I cried out but my cries were muffled by her mouth, still on mine. I held onto her, squeezing, until my body became still. While my hands languished in her soft breasts and stiffened nipples, she pushed herself against me. Slipping her hands under my t-shirt, she ran her palms up and down my spine. Our mouths separated. As she leaned her head back, I licked and bit the sleek taut skin of her neck until she whimpered.

Then, with unbridled lust, I tore her blouse off in one great tug, sending the buttons flying. Her bra fell away and I dragged her down into the mud, smearing the gooey stuff all over her chest. She watched me, her face open and wanting. Then she brought my muddy hands up to her face and placed them on her cheeks. She pulled my t-shirt off over my head and I lay on top of her, my breasts slipping and sliding against hers. A moan came from her, and I bent my head and took her lips again.

As my tongue filled her throat, my entire weight descended on her. The sensation of her under me, squishing in the mud, writhing in passion, brought my yearning flesh, again, to release. I pulled my mouth away from hers and groaned, "Oh, Joanne," as my muscles gradually ceased their twittering.

My orgasm seemed to ignite her as she opened herself wide, pushed up hard against me, and crooned, "Oh, Sidney, I love you."

Her sweet declaration revived me and I yanked her jeans off. She lay naked in the puddle, and as I examined her she wriggled under my intense glare. I pushed her legs open, and scooping up some mud, I spread it over her genitals, stroking her labia. She moved to the rhythm of my touch, her gasps becoming groans.

I pulled off my jeans, climbed on her again, and pressed my hipbone hard into her slippery cunt. Her moans grew louder as I ground furiously into her gaping, mud-caked loins. Fluid poured out of her, mixing with the mud.

Suddenly, she bucked and cried out, "Yes, oh yes!" Then she emitted a prolonged howl that shattered my ear. I clung to her, feeling her pulsate with the violent orgasm, as the current raged throughout every feverish fiber of her body.

The sun had been out for some time when I shifted myself off of Joanne. We sat up and looked at each other. Spontaneously, we both started to giggle, then laughed uproariously. I was giddy, dizzy with joy at the sight of our muddy selves.

"We'd better find our clothes," I suggested when I finally caught my breath. We dug around the puddle until we found the necessary items.

"Yuck!" Joanne uttered, squinching her face as she held up her blouse and pants dripping with globs of mud.

I looked around and suddenly realized that I didn't know exactly where we were. "We're somewhere on the edge of the Loxihattchee swamp," I said. "We ran pretty far." However, I was relieved that we weren't in somebody's backyard. Joanne was busy trying to squeeze herself into her sopping clothes; I started to do the same.

We crawled out of the ditch and headed back toward my house. We walked in silence. I knew we needed to talk, but didn't know how to begin. I was still feeling lightheaded. After a few minutes, we looked at each other and burst into laughter again.

"That ditch will forever be known as our love swamp," Joanne said, grinning.

"Yeah," I acknowledged, noting that she had used that word again — "love." "Joanne, I've been in love with you from the moment I saw you," I blurted out.

"Sidney, I'm so glad. I thought you hated me, the way you avoided me. I've also loved you — from the beginning —although at first, I wasn't exactly sure what my feelings meant. I mean, I knew I had a crush on you, but

I thought maybe it had something to do with your being the pastor. After a while, though, the feelings were so deep and constant that I had to recognize them for what they were — sexual. Even so, I didn't know what to do about it. You didn't seem to feel the same way, and besides, I've never been with a woman before. Have you?"

"Yeah, once in seminary. But that doesn't make it any easier for me; I've known about my attraction to women for a long time. It's complicated too because I really am a very spiritual person, and I can't seem to put this together with that. Oh, let's not think about that right now." I stopped walking and turned toward her. "I want so much to be with you, Joanne. It seems like I've always wanted that."

Joanne took my face in her hands. "Sidney, I want that too, more than anything I've ever wanted." An urgency to wallow again in her flesh sprung up in me. I wanted to make love to her forever. We hastened to my house.

Just as the parsonage came into view we saw a car coming down the road toward us. As it neared I recognized, with some relief, that it was Win. She pulled up next to us and stuck her head out of the window. "What the heck have you two been doing — mud wrestling?" The shock and bewilderment on her face was enough to get us laughing again. She finally gave up, realizing that she wasn't going to get a reasonable explanation out of us. "I have to get away from these church people," she muttered. "I'm glad you two are all right. That's the main thing," she shouted as she drove off. I thought I saw her smile.

When we reached the parsonage, I held the door open for Joanne and noticed her bra hanging from her back pocket. Once inside, I asked her as seriously as I could: "What's that hanging out of your back pocket?" She reached back and pulled out the bedraggled thing.

"Oh, my God, do you think Win saw it?" she asked, blushing profusely.

"I have no idea," I squealed, breaking into giggles as tears ran down my face.

By the time we recovered from our last bout of hysterics, we were sitting on the living room floor. I still couldn't quite believe that she was there with me. We crawled toward each other and collapsed in each other's arms. As we kissed, the passion rose in us again.

"I don't think I'll ever be able to get enough of you," I said when our lips parted.

"Why don't you just try," she challenged, lifting my t-shirt and taking my breast in her mouth. We rolled our way into the bedroom, where we burned in our love for hours.

Later that night as we lay quietly in the dark I asked, "By the way, who's that man you've been with lately — the dark curly-haired one?"

"That's my brother. He's visiting me from up north. I've been trying to introduce him to you all week, but you wouldn't stay put long enough."

"Your brother?"

"Yeah."

"Oh brother!"

"What?"

"Never mind."

❧

Dawn was just breaking when we dozed off. I awoke to the sun streaming through the slats of my jalousie windows. I looked over at Joanne sleeping peacefully. My heart swelled with overpowering joy as I watched her. I was amazed that this wonderful creature lay here, in my bed. Life seemed suddenly easy.

I moved toward Joanne and kissed her lightly. Her eyes opened. "I'm sorry, I didn't mean to wake you," I whispered.

"Umm," she moaned, and put her arms around me.

Within moments we were stirred again. Even after a night of lovemaking, just her touch was enough to bring out all that lovely sensuality in me. She, too, pricked up so easily to the touch of my hands, my lips. Her breasts popped out to my command. Her skin stood up in bumps. Tiny tremors rippled through her belly, down to her instantly soaked genitalia. We floated, yet one more time, in our erotic joining.

In the afterglow, reality began to reassert itself. "I think I should call Win and tell her I won't be coming in today."

Joanne jumped up, opening her eyes wide. "Oh, gosh, I have to call work. What should I say? I know, I'll tell them something personal has come up and I can't make it in."

I got up first and called the church office. Win answered the phone. "Win?"

"Hi, Sid."

"Hi. Listen, I'm going to take today off."

"Well, that's a first!" she said. "You deserve it. Have fun. And Sid?"

"Yeah?"

"Stay out of the mud!"

"Okay, Win, I'll try." I chuckled. "I wonder if she knows," I said, half to myself, as I climbed back into bed.

"Who, Win?" Joanne asked. "She is pretty perceptive."

"Perceptive! I swear the woman can read my mind!"

"If that's the case, she must be having a good time," Joanne shot back, and laughed.

"Well, I guess it's my turn." Joanne got out of bed to make her call. Stomach pains reminded me that we hadn't eaten in a very long time. I went to check the refrigerator and dragged out some cheese, fruit, butter, and milk. I put some English muffins in the toaster and started some coffee. I returned to the bedroom with a tray full of food. "Breakfast in bed, my dear?"

"I'm starving! I didn't even realize it till now," Joanne replied with enthusiasm.

After we devoured what was on the tray, I got up to get the coffee. We lounged against the headboard and sipped pensively. My problem, though temporarily obliterated, was not solved; I still had God to contend with. Joanne saw the concern creep into my face. "Something wrong?" she asked, gently.

I wanted to be honest with her, but I didn't want to frighten her. "It's this spiritual problem. Umm ... you know ... about us and God. See, I'm not sure that what we're doing isn't wrong — not that I could give you up now, anyway."

"You'd better not!" she said emphatically.

I saw fear in her face and leaned over to kiss her. "Don't worry. Now that we're together, I can't imagine life without you. I'll just have to work this out somehow."

Joanne was quiet for a while; then she spoke: "When I was a kid I went to church camp. And every summer, especially as I got older, I would inevitably fall in love with one of the female counselors. But I didn't realize that's what it was. I always thought I was having a deep religious experience."

I nodded. "Yeah, I know what you mean."

"When I grew up I realized that those feelings came more from my glands than they did from God. But thinking about it now — maybe it was a little of both."

I knew what she meant. In my heart I too felt that what Joanne and I had, though sexual, was also somehow spiritual. Instead of feeling like we were doing something wrong, it felt very special, like a great gift — the gift of a love that encompassed all of me.

Joanne went on: "God gave us this need for sexual expression and gave us this way of being close to each other. What we have, to me anyway, is already way more satisfying than any relationship I've ever had before. How can it be wrong? But, I guess you're not going to get an unbiased opinion from me."

"Maybe not," I acknowledged, "but still, what you're saying has a ring of truth."

"Of course, the church doesn't see it that way," Joanne added.

"Oh, hang the church," I said, with some disgust. "To tell you the truth, I don't really worry about a bunch of rules and regulations that men — the patriarchs — have created because of their need to control people. That's the way I see most of any church's dogmas. My relationship is with God. I get my direction from God and Christ, not the church. Of course, I don't get on people's cases who want to live by those dogmas. That's their choice. In my work as pastor, I just make sure that the people in my care don't lose sight of their own relationship with a loving God — that they learn to make that a priority over the organization of the Church. That's my mission."

"Amen, sister," Joanne shouted out, clapping.

"It is to God that I am responsible, and to God I must go for an answer — tomorrow. For today, let's just enjoy ourselves!"

"Amen again, sister!" Joanne moved over to me seductively and took away my coffee cup. And enjoy ourselves we did!

XI

Early the next morning, before going to the office I went into the church sanctuary to meditate; I had a lot to discuss with God. The place was dark except for the early morning sunlight coming in through the east side windows, and the air was cool and damp. I settled myself in the pew, my feet flat on the floor and my back straight. I held out my hands, palms up, and took several deep, slow breaths. Immediately I connected with the stillness and peace in the room and began to pray:

"God, a long time ago I made a commitment to You. It is a commitment which I have reaffirmed daily since that time. It's a commitment to work towards knowing You better. It's a commitment to work towards turning my life over to You for complete direction and guidance. It's a commitment most of all, to seek You first above all other things."

The words of a verse we often used in church ran through my mind: Seek ye first the presence of God, and God's righteousness, and all these things shall be added unto you. "God, I do not wish to abandon my commitment to You if, in fact, I even could. As much as I love Joanne and want so desperately to be with her, You still must come first. Without You, I would be like branches without a tree. This I know to be true."

I began to tremble all over, and tears started down my cheeks. I knew God was there, but I was afraid of what I may have to do. I continued my prayer:

"At this time, I am searching for Your answer. I have given up the struggle, and I have allowed a person into my life, perhaps in a way which is wrong in Your eyes. I need to know if this kind of relationship is right, and if this relationship is Your will for me. In my heart it feels so right, so good. But can I trust myself in this? I just don't know. Please, show me the way."

I remained in the sanctuary for a while, until the tremors and the tears stopped. Then I looked around. The birds were still singing outside, the crickets humming. Broiling air blew through the room. Sunlight shone through the windows onto the cross hanging over the altar and played on the smooth wood, flickering and dancing in the breeze. It made an image like the flame of a candle, and for a moment I was hypnotized by this reflection. Finally I got up, walked into my office, and sat down at my desk quietly, still somewhat in my trance.

Win barged into my space. "Oh!" she shrieked, clutching at her chest. "Sidney, you scared me. I didn't hear you come in."

"Sorry, Win. I'm in kind of a quiet mood today."

She stared at me pointedly, then pulled up a chair close to me and sat down. "Are you ever going to talk to me about this?"

"Yes, Win, I am," I answered. Then I tried to tell her everything, but the words would not come easily. "I — uh — I'm in — um — I had — "

"You're in love with Joanne," she said, impatiently.

I looked at her in astonishment.

"Come on — I wasn't born yesterday, you know. When I saw you two together the other day, I knew. And even before that, the chemistry between you two was always so thick, you could have cut it with a knife. So, what's the problem?"

"Win, she's a woman."

"I hope it didn't take you too long to figure that out. I thought it was kind of obvious, myself," she chuckled.

"Oh, you know what I mean." I smiled back at her.

"Look, Sidney, in my book, love is love. And how people express their love is their business. Does it make you happy?"

"Oh, yes."

"Are you honest with her?"

"Of course."

"Are you hurting anyone?"

"No."

"Well, then, mazel tov!"

"It's God I'm worried about."

"God? Honey, I think God can take care of Himself — or Herself, if you wish."

"Do you think a relationship like this is right in God's eyes?"

"Oh, you'll have to ask God about that."

"I have, and all I know is that I feel more spiritual than ever — complete. It's like a piece of me that was missing has finally been put into place. But the line is that God disapproves."

"The line from where?" Win asked. "Other people? The Bible? Just what does the Bible say?"

"Win, I've pored over all those sections that people say are the antihomosexual ones, and I can't find anything in them that really speaks to the issue at all. The one about Sodom and Gomorrah — I see a bunch of angry, hostile men wanting to rape those other men. That's about rape, humiliation, inhospitality. Another section lists men sleeping with men along with not eating pork or lobster and the killing of divorced people who get married again. You know, those old-time laws that have to do with the health issues of the times. And finally, something in Romans about women doing unnatural acts — what does that mean? Being with Joanne feels as natural to me as breathing."

"You know what I think?" Win broke in. "I think you ought to start listening to yourself. You're a person who embraces life with gusto. You enjoy all the gifts that God has given you. Why don't you just accept this one and stop throwing it back in God's face."

"Maybe you're right," I mumbled.

"You think about it a little while." Win got up from her chair. "I've got to run to the store for a minute. I'll be back." She went into her office and moments later, I heard her walk out the back door. I noticed that she had left the door between our offices open. I leaned back in my chair. I'll bet she *is* an angel, I mused.

All of a sudden I heard a voice coming from Win's office. Was it the voice of God? It was *my* voice:

I challenge every one of you today to let the love of God into your life, to own for yourself what God freely gives, to open yourself to the light and power that is yours. Know that you are loved — not because of what you do, but because of who you are. And who are you? You are God's child. As you go through this week, turn off your mind when it starts to tell you that you don't deserve God's love. Open your heart! Be assured as you live your life, from the small daily tasks to the large heavy burdens, that God is with you. God is with you in everything — simply because you are a child of God.

Myths and legends

We had spent the day at the beach, had dinner at a great seafood restaurant that overlooked the bay, and finished off the evening dancing at the Pied Piper. When we finally made our way back to the lesbian-owned guest house, we were still pretty wound up. It was late, but excited about our Provincetown vacation and thrilled that all eight of us had managed to be there together, we couldn't let the day end.

We were gathered in the nice large living room laughing and making small talk, when Sabra said, "Hey, I have an idea!" We all stopped talking.

"What, Sab?" several of us asked, in hopeful anticipation of an adventure.

"Let's play Mythology," she answered.

"What's that?" Myra bravely asked. Everyone else was looking at Sabra blankly.

"None of you have ever played Mythology?" she asked in disbelief.

We all looked at each other, then back at her. "No, what is it?"

"Oh, wow," Sabra screeched. "This is going to be great! It goes like this: Everybody tries to think of a lesbian myth — you know, things that straight people think about us. But if you come up with a myth, you have to tell a story supporting it, you know, as if it were true."

Poor Ursula immediately stuck her foot in her mouth. "You mean like all straight people think that lesbians really want to be men and have pricks and all that?"

"Exactly!" Sabra said, jumping up from her chair. She pointed her finger at Ursula. "Now, you have to tell a story about that, as if it were true."

We all started chuckling, warming to the idea. "Yeah, come on, Ursula, tell us a story," someone urged. Instinctively we moved off our chairs to sit on the floor in a circle. Ursula remained in her chair, her face straining as her mind went to work.

We were an impatient lot, and after allowing her only a few moments to think, we started badgering her. "Come on, that's long enough." "Out with it."

A smile finally broke out on Ursula's face. She rose out of her chair and came to sit on the floor in the center of our circle. We moved in closer, readying ourselves for her story.

"Okay," Ursula began, "all lesbians want to have pricks and would do just about anything to get one."

When I was first coming out in New York, I didn't know anyone in the community. I had no lesbian friends, so I decided to start going to lesbian activities to meet women. I called the Lesbian Switchboard and asked for a list of things going on. I ruled out the bars and the dances; I thought it would be easier to meet people at a gathering like a women's poetry reading, or a concert.

The woman at the switchboard told me about a group that met weekly and that would be especially good for someone just coming out. She said this group would get me started in the right direction. The name of it was the H.T.G.A.P. Creative Seminars. I asked her what the letters stood for. She said, "It'll be obvious when you get there. And," she added before we hung up, "this group will satisfy some of your deepest needs." Wow, I thought. I was convinced.

That Friday night I put on my best jeans and went to the H.T.G.A.P. Creative Seminar with much anticipation. When I arrived, I was surprised to find myself in a very large auditorium filled to capacity with women of all ages. The crowd had an attitude of eagerness; voices around me were hushed in excited murmurings; and there was energy in the air. A great big sign hung above the stage displaying the letters: H.T.G.A.P. After finally getting a seat and settling in, I realized that there was going to be a speaker. I was dying to find out what this was all about.

Suddenly the lights dimmed to darkness and the crowd became silent. A beam flashed on the stage and a woman walked out to the podium. She was all butched out and I could swear that I saw a huge lump in her jeans by the crotch. When she reached center stage she lifted her arms up high, and the crowd went wild with applause and cheers. The woman waved, returning the greeting.

When the masses were quiet again the woman spoke. "Welcome, everyone — newcomers and old friends — to: Have to Get a Prick Creative Seminars. I am Penelope Johnson."

Oh my God, I said to myself, stunned. But after all, I had been out for several months and knew it was time to start looking for my penis. I had to face the fact, at that moment, that I had shamefully been putting off that task.

The speaker continued: "Good news tonight, lesbians of America. Good news especially for those who have not yet found a suitable prosthesis and for those who are not happy with their current dicks. The word *pre-dick-a-ment* takes on new meaning today!" The crowd was leaning forward, all ears. Not a sound could be heard in the hall.

"As some of you know, I've been in constant touch with the organization O.R.G.A.N." There was a blast of applause. "For you newcomers, that's the Organization for Reusable Genitalia Additions Now." There was more applause and bravos from the crowd. "They have recently informed me that our search for that perfect schlong is over!" The crowd started to go wild again, and Penelope held up her hands to shush them. "They have informed me that legislation is about to be passed that will require all men to donate their genitals upon death for transplant. Special coolers are being set up right now for the purpose of gathering up the withering wangs of the recently deceased."

The crowd was crazed with excitement. Women jumped up and down screaming, crying, hugging each other, and furiously rubbing their crotches.

Penelope silenced them again. "Furthermore, they are pursuing legislation regarding the collection of wieners in question. This would mean that the man may not have to be completely dead before special crews of lesbian medical technicians rush to lop off the much-needed cocks."

"So, sisters, I tell you tonight: as the cards are being passed out, please put in your requests now — name, address, size, and color desired. And please, ladies, let's be realistic — we can't all have twelve-inchers!" She paused a moment and scanned the crowd slowly with serious eyes, like a mother disciplining her children. "Don't forget to write down whether you want it hard or soft, and please don't forget to fill in the space about circumcision. This is very, very important — many a poor pecker has been ruined by women who try to remove the unwanted foreskin themselves."

Then Penelope made her final potent point. "It could be any day now that a medical tech will be knocking on your door with that very special beer cooler in hand."

The lights came back on and cards were passed around. I filled mine out carefully, thrilled that so early in my lesbian life I was going to get what I had so desperately wanted — a real penie! How blessed I was.

Before we dispersed on that monumental night, Penelope Johnson left us with a new reality. "Lesbians of the world, I promise you that before the end of another decade there will not be a lesbian among us sans her throbbing membrane. Very soon we will all be walking around and living our lives with that very precious bulge alive in our pants."

The jubilant crowd raved out of control and the place rocked with joy as our leader and savior, Penelope Johnson, slowly left the stage. She exited waving her upraised arms, with the middle finger on each hand extended in triumph.

❧

Ursula ended her story with true solemnity. The seven of us convulsed on the floor in laughter. "That was too much!" Janet spit out. "Let's do another one."

"Wait," Susan pleaded. "I can't take any more right now."

Ursula looked appropriately pleased with herself. Sabra was awestruck. "Ursula, that was terrific!" she complimented. "Who wants to go next?"

"I doubt anybody can top that!" Myra groaned, lying on her back and holding her stomach.

Then everyone grew quiet, and I imagined I could hear the wheels turning in our brains. There were lots of myths about us; that part was easy. But who would dare to be the next one to come up with a story?

"Um..." a small utterance came from Susan. Our eyes immediately turned toward her. "Well, I remember a pretty wild accusation that was made about the gay community by one of those TV evangelists a while ago."

"Yeah?" we sang out in unison.

"I was watching TV about a year ago and this Billy Boobey something-or-other was preaching to a packed auditorium. He told them that New York City was the sin capital of the world. He said that in New York homosexuals kidnap heterosexuals and hold them until they're brainwashed into becoming gay."

"Get out of here!" Judy interrupted in disbelief.

"It's true," Susan defended. "And that's not all. This preacher said that he actually knew a man that this had happened to. And he warned his congregation to stay away from the city!"

Sabra was satisfied. "Okay, that counts. Now, Suz, tell us a story that proves that myth to be true."

Susan took her place in the middle of the circle. She sat there for a few minutes, thinking while we waited, staring at her. Her face became increasingly brighter as the story came together in her mind. "Okay, I'm ready," she announced. "All homosexuals in New York kidnap heterosexuals for the purpose of brainwashing them into becoming gay."

❧

It was Friday afternoon and the gang was gathering at the underground clubhouse in the Village. It was gang headquarters for S.W.I.T.C.H. — Sappho's Womyn's Initiative to Change Heterosexuals. The clubhouse was a large dark basement filled with torturing devices used to effect the complete change of sexual orientation from hetero to homo.

The gay men had their own version. They called their club A.N.U.S. — the Association of Newly Uninvited Sexuality. They did their thing separately from the women. The two groups met annually at a big conference — you know, to discuss new techniques and progress, and do some general networking. The conference was called F.U.C.K. — Fellowship of Unbelievably Callous Kidnappers.

Anyway, that Friday night as the members of S.W.I.T.C.H. were arriving one by one, their leader Mickey studied a map of New York City that was laid out on a table. At exactly 5 p.m. she started the meeting, giving the gang their instructions for the evening. "Okay, everybody, listen up." She began to pace, formulating the night's plan in her head. Mick was a huge, heavy woman, and completely leather. Chains hung from her motorcycle jacket. She packed a big S.W.I.T.C.H. blade; it was the symbol of the club. (Everyone had the insignia — a big open blade with blood dripping from it, with the letters S.W.I.T.C.H. over the top of it — sewn on the backs of their jackets.) Her blonde hair was greased back tight, with an orange streak running down the middle and culminating in a long orange tail in the back. She never smiled, with one exception — whenever the gang was successful in completing a sexual switch, a smile would crease her face. Brainwashing heterosexuals was her life's mission.

"This is the plan for tonight, guys," Mickey continued. "Get it now! There's no time for questions, and absolutely no time for mistakes." Gang members who were lying around on the broken-down furniture picked up their heads to be sure they caught every word.

"Ronnie, I want you to take Blazer and cover the George Washington Bridge. Zero, you and Ziggie take the Brooklyn Bridge. Hank and Dasher — the Verrazano. I'm covering the Lincoln Tunnel with Tommie and Lou. I've got my sights set on a suburban housewife for tonight."

"Yeah," Ronnie agreed, nodding. "Their minds are already mush from all the vacuuming and soap operas."

"Right," Mickey said. "And easier to mold — our way!" She drew out the words. Low grunts, chuckles, and nods came from the others.

"What about us?" Rosita asked.

"You know the rules," Mickey said. "No fluffs go out on the grabs. It's too dangerous and we have to move fast. The cops are on to us and we may be spotted."

"Oh, that's bull!" Belinda blurted out angrily. "The cops are scared shit of you and you know it."

"Listen, doll." Mickey was getting pissed. "I'm not into anything going wrong tonight. I want a good score. Don't forget we messed up last week when Ronnie grabbed that transvestite — dumb dyke."

"Look," Ronnie yelled, "I've already apologized for that a million times. She could've fooled anyone."

"That's true," Ziggie said in her friend's defense. "She was very hot. How could we know she was a man?"

"Just forget about it," Mickey ordered. "I just don't want any more surprises like that again. I'm still shook up from getting a handful of cock."

"Ugh!" the gang moaned.

"Let's get moving, bikers," Mickey commanded. "We've got to get into position. Girls, set up while we're gone. Get the cattle prod and the electrodes ready. Films set up. I'll decide what to start with as soon as we know what we've got. And ladies, get lots of diet food in case we're lucky enough to grab a housewife. And lots of diet chocolate ice cream."

"We know all that," Cindy barked. "Just go on."

"How about a little kiss for luck, gorgeous?" Mickey asked with a wink.

Cindy slinked over and planted a wet one on Mickey's lips. "Maybe you'll get the rest later," Cindy cooed as she seductively ran her hands over Mickey's leathered ass.

"Ooo..." the gang chirped.

"All right, womyn, let's get to work!" Mickey shouted enthusiastically. Ronnie, Blaze, Zero, Ziggie, Hank, Dasher, Tommie, Lou, and Mickey strutted their stuff out of the clubhouse and onto the street, where their Harleys awaited them. They climbed onto the bikes and sat revving their motors for a few minutes. Their anticipation rose to a peak with the roars and vibrations of the macho machines under them. When Mickey gave the sign to move, they peeled off down the street.

Mickey, Lou, and Tommie sped to their spot at the Lincoln Tunnel. Arriving at the tunnel's exit into the city, they pulled their bikes off to the side of the road and scanned the incoming traffic. Mickey picked up her bike phone and called the others, checking positions. Everything was set. The gang sat back in their places waiting for the arrival of their mark. They kept the motors running on the bikes, revving them up every now and then for effect. Tommie had an incredible eye for housewives, and Mickey had total confidence in her ability. So, while Tommie leered into the oncoming cars, Mickey and Lou relaxed and cruised for dykes.

After about half an hour, Tommie hollered, "That's it!" She pointed to a Volvo station wagon that had just come through the tunnel. The three churned their bikes up to a blast and leapt into the traffic.

"What we got?" Mickey called out.

"A housewife and her husband," Tommie called back.

"Great!" Mickey beamed. Her blue eyes narrowed into a glare. The gang maneuvered themselves right behind the Volvo.

Their presence did not go unnoticed by the people in the car. "Sam, are those Hell's Angels behind us?" the woman asked.

Sam looked in his rearview mirror. He raised an eyebrow as he said in macho abandon, "Probably. Just don't look at them," he instructed.

The woman was nervous, however, and couldn't help but check on the bikers, periodically catching a glimpse of them in the side-view mirror. "Sam," she asked, after a few more of those glimpses, "you don't think they could be those homos we've heard about, do you?"

"God no, Melissa," Sam responded impatiently. "How could they be homos? It's eight o'clock on a Friday night. The homos are still home putting on their makeup and picking out their dresses for the evening."

"I'm not talking about the men," Melissa said slowly.

Sam's face suddenly lost its color as he quickly checked his rearview mirror again. "Oh, my God, you might be right!" he said, half to himself.

Melissa covered her face. "Oh no, I knew we shouldn't have come to the city," she groaned into her hands.

"It was your idea!" Sam screamed at her. "You had to come to New York. I wanted to see the Matawan players at the mall. But no! You had to see a Broadway play."

"What are we going to do?" Melissa cried beseechingly, as her terror grew.

"Nothing," Sam said, as if he had the situation well in hand. "They're probably not even after us. And maybe they're not homos."

"Please, God, let them be Hell's Angels," Melissa cried pleadingly.

When they stopped at a red light, Mickey roared her chopper up to the driver's side of the car. She wanted some information, and she knew the woman would never open her window. The man would have to act brave — he would open his window.

Mickey turned her head toward Sam and stared at him. He looked at her quickly out of the corner of his eye, then snapped his head straight ahead again. Mickey knocked on the car window. He turned his head back and met her eyes. Mickey saw raw fear in his face. She gave him a phoney smile and motioned for him to open his window. He did so, but cracked it only a couple of inches.

"Yeah?" he said, unable to hide a quiver in his voice.

"Welcome to New York," Mickey said. Sam just nodded. "Just think of us as the Welcome Wagon," she continued, laughing at her own joke. Sam didn't think it was funny. When Mickey finally collected herself she asked, "Where you from?"

"New Jersey," Sam spit out.

"Ah, nice place, Jersey. Any particular part?" Mickey couldn't stop herself from being a little sarcastic.

"Matawan," Sam offered.

"Mat-a-wan," she said, drawing the word out. "That's some bad place!" Mickey broke into laughter again, unable to control her glee.

Sam rolled his window back up. Melissa was rocking back and forth in the passenger's seat with her face still buried in her hands, and emitting little nervous squeaks.

"Melissa, calm down," Sam snapped. His shaky voice was not too consoling, however. "We'll just drive to a parking garage near the theater, park the car, and walk quickly into the theater. Don't worry."

Mickey dropped back to join the others. She was sure now. This was it! She picked up her bike phone and called in the troops. When she made the call to Hank and Dasher, no one answered right away and there was a lot of static on the line. "Hank! Dasher!" Mickey called over and over.

Finally Hank responded. "Some trouble here, Boss."

"What?" Mickey asked, alarmed.

"We were watching cars at our spot near the Verrazano, when a woman jumped out of a car coming over the bridge. She started running toward us, screaming, 'Take me! Take me!' We tried to split but she was on us too fast. She attached herself to Dasher and the bike, and before we knew what was going on, she threw her arms around Dasher's neck and hung on desperately. She was squeezing Dasher's throat so tight that Dasher started choking. She begged us, 'Take me — please! I want to go.'

Finally I pulled her off and we peeled out as fast as we could. She actually started chasing us on foot, screaming over and over: 'I want to be a lesbian!' Then Dasher threw out a bunch of bar fliers that she had in her bag. When I last looked back, the woman had stopped chasing us and was frantically picking up those fliers. Then she started jumping up and down with both hands full of fliers, laughing hysterically. We're okay now. Dasher's just a little freaked out."

"Okay, okay, you did good," Mickey commended. "Now get to the theater district. We'll meet you there. We're onto one!"

"Right, Mick," Hank responded.

"Poor kids," Mickey mumbled, shaking her head. She turned to Lou and Tommie. "Hank and Dasher just had a pretty terrifying experience — an attack!" She looked at the ground somberly.

"Oh no, not that!" Lou said.

"Afraid so," Mickey said. "But they'll be okay. Come on, let's concentrate on what we've got to do."

They saw the Volvo slip into a parking garage. While they waited at the garage exit, the rest of the gang came rumbling up two by two to join them. When Sam and Melissa came walking out of the parking garage, the nine gang members slowly rode up next to the couple.

Sam turned toward the gang and stopped, his face white as a ghost. "Look," he said, "we don't want any trouble. I just don't want to become a homosexual. Not right now, anyway."

"Man, we don't want you," Mickey responded incredulously. "We want your wife. Just for a few hours."

"Oh, is that all," Sam said, looking relieved.

"Sam?!" Melissa screeched.

"Oh!" Sam stuck out his chin and hardened his eyes. "Yeah, what do you mean by a few hours?"

"We'll let her go some time tonight."

Sam nodded. "Uh-huh."

"Sam?!" Melissa screamed even louder.

"Well, honey, it's not so unreasonable."

Melissa started to faint. Ziggie jumped off her bike and caught the falling woman. She dragged the sagging body over to her bike and lifted her up onto it. "Hold tight, sweet face," Ziggie instructed the half-conscious woman.

Melissa hung limply onto Ziggie as the gang roared off, leaving Sam in the dust. Mickey looked back at him. He was waving. "Bye-bye, Melissa!" Mickey heard him call out as they sped away with their catch.

The gang carried their woman du jour into the underground clubhouse. The girls had done their jobs well; everything was set up to go. Ronnie and Blazer dumped Melissa into a big stuffed chair and Mickey rushed over with smelling salts. Melissa's mind cleared. "What are you going to do to me?" she screamed, looking around the room. When her eyes came to rest on a huge wall poster of one woman fucking another with a huge black dildo, she fainted again. Mickey was quick with the smelling salts and soon had her revived again.

"Look, Melissa," Mick said, exasperated. "This is going to be a drag if you keep fainting. If you lose consciousness, I can't be responsible for what these dykes might do."

"You mean, you'll rape me?" Melissa howled.

"Of course not," Mickey said. "All I mean is that we might start lusting after your body."

"I'll stay awake — I'll stay awake," Melissa insisted immediately, her eyes now wide open.

"Try to relax now, sweet pea. Here, have some diet chocolate ice cream." Rosita rushed over with a big bowl.

"Oh. Okay," Melissa said, brightening. She grabbed the bowl out of Rosita's hands and dove into the stuff.

Mickey called the gang together for a conference. In their meeting she paced. "I don't know about Melissa — she's such a featherhead. Are we sure we want her?" She took a long drag off her cigarette.

"Mick," Ronnie said, surprised, "I can't believe you said that! You know you can't tell what kind of a dyke she'll be. Remember that real mousey broad we did last year? She's got her own gang on the Lower East Side now."

"Yeah, yeah — you're right," Mick agreed. "I must be tired." She rubbed her hands together. "Okay, let's start her off with the TV films."

Cindy looked at Mickey questioningly. "You mean all the movies ever made for TV about male serial killers slaughtering women? There's too many of them. It would take a week. A month!"

"Of course I don't mean all of them. Just pick out three or four and show them to her all at the same time."

Cindy put it together, and soon Melissa had four big TV screens in front of her. She gasped and groaned at the continuous images of men brutally killing women.

When the films were over, she was spent, pale, and had bags under her eyes.

"So, what do you think of men now?" Mick asked Melissa as she stood in front of her picking her teeth with a toothpick.

"Well," Melissa answered sheepishly, "those were sick men." The gang murmured to themselves. "What are you saying?" Melissa asked, turning toward them. "Are they talking about me?" she asked Mickey.

"No, nothing," Mickey reassured her. "Don't pay any attention to them. Okay, now we're going to get a little more active."

Blazer and Hank hustled over and reached up under Melissa's dress. "What are you doing? Stop it!" Melissa commanded, swatting at them.

"Now, now, just be patient," Mickey consoled her. She grabbed Melissa's arms at the wrists and held them motionless. Hank put a tiny electrode down Melissa's underpants until it came to rest on her cunt. As soon as Mickey let go of her hands, Melissa pulled at the electrode. But before she could yank it out, Blazer pushed a button and there was a buzzing sound. Melissa began wiggling in her chair.

"Oh! Oh! Oh!" she cried out, shuddering from head to toe. "What was that?" she asked with a funny smile on her face. The gang members looked at each other.

"Just as I suspected," Ronnie said.

Mickey explained. "That was an orgasm."

"Oh. So *that's* what they feel like," Melissa said, grinning. "Do it again."

"All in good time, my dear," Mick said.

Next, Blazer put a cattle prod against Melissa's ass and another buzz was heard. "Ouch!" Melissa howled. "That hurt!" Just as she was about to stand up, the clit electrode was buzzed again. "Unh — oh — unh — wonderful," Melissa moaned, slumping back into her chair.

Mick told her she'd have an orgasm approximately every five minutes for a while. "Think you can take it?" Mick asked her.

"Absolutely!" Melissa said excitedly.

"Start the film," Mick ordered. Belinda put on a video of women making love to other women. Every five minutes the orgasm electrode was buzzed. Melissa oohed and ahhed, shivering and smiling through the movie. Afterwards she was given another dish of diet chocolate ice cream. She had relaxed considerably.

Belinda now set up two televisions in front of Melissa. One played a video of a heterosexual couple making love; the other showed one of lesbians making love. Whenever the lesbian movie was turned on, the orgasm electrode buzzed. When Belinda switched to the heterosexual one, the cattle prod was set off. Faster and faster these alternations were made, until the gang could hear continuous verbal emissions from Melissa: "Ooh ... ahh — ouch! Ooh ... ahh — ouch!" The gang members couldn't control their giggling.

An hour later, Mick said, "Okay, enough."

"Oh, please don't stop," Melissa begged.

"Which video do you want?" Mick asked, chuckling.

"The lesbians, the lesbians — more lesbians," Melissa pleaded.

"Maybe later," Mickey told her. "Let's give her a little rest," Mickey instructed the gang. "Show her the housewife movie."

For the next hour Melissa watched a housewife clean a big ranch-style house, doing mostly laundry, vacuuming, and cleaning bathrooms. While she watched the film, the gang forced her to eat Weight Watchers entrées.

When Mickey went to inspect their prisoner, Melissa was exhibiting symptoms of severe depression. "Stop the film!" Mickey ordered. She took the half-eaten plates of diet food away from Melissa, who was staring off into space with food hanging out of her mouth. Mickey grabbed her shoulders and shook her hard. "Melissa! Say something." Finally, Melissa muttered, "I need a drink."

Relieved, Mickey said to Ziggie, "That housewife film is heavy-duty stuff. I'm thinking of getting rid of it."

"Yeah," Ziggie nodded. "One of these days somebody isn't going to snap out of that dazed depression it puts them in. Maybe there's some weird chemicals in that diet food garbage?"

"I wouldn't doubt it," Mickey said as she looked at Melissa, who had closed her mouth and was pulling her dress up looking for the clit electrode. "How can I turn this thing on?" she asked.

"Melissa." Mickey walked over to her. "Now we have something for you that will definitely brighten your spirits."

It was the pièce de résistance. Melissa was given a tray with assorted flavors of frozen yogurt and the book *Rubyfruit Jungle.* When she finished reading and eating, she was given a tray of various fruits and cheeses and the book *Rapture and the Second Coming*. When these were consumed, she was given a large bowl of real chocolate ice cream and shown the film *Desert Hearts*.

After all these things were done, Mickey, Ronnie, and Rosita took Melissa into a small private room. After a few minutes Mickey stuck her head out of the door and said, "Get me a pan of boiling water, lots of clean towels, a pair of sharp scissors, and some mousse." Belinda and Cindy rushed to comply.

The gang members paced anxiously as they waited outside the small room. Finally, after what seemed to them an eternity, Mickey emerged. She had stripped down to her leather undershirt and was drying her hands with a towel. A big toothy grin crept over her wide face as she announced, "It's a boy!" The gang broke into cheers and laughter. Then, abruptly, the noise stopped.

Everyone stood motionless and wide-eyed as they watched Melissa emerge from the little room. She sauntered over to where the gang was huddled together, her hands shoved into the pockets of her shaggy jeans. Her face had been scrubbed clean of all makeup, her breasts bounced freely under a tight-fitting cotton muscle shirt, and a red bandana was tied around her neck. Her hair had been cut short and was greased back, with a small braided tail hanging down the back. She turned to the gang, whose mouths hung open as they stared at her in amazement, and said: "Call me Mel."

❧

Susan stood up and took a bow as we clapped, cheered, and made declarations of admiration.

The sun was rising. Those so unwilling to go to bed a few hours before were now ready to drop. Sabra asked, "Well, what do you think of the game?" The group unanimously acknowledged feelings of great enthusiasm, but exhaustion had definitely set in.

Judy said, "I have a myth."

We shook our heads sleepily, trying to force wakefulness into our tired brains, still unwilling to miss anything.

"The myth is that all lesbians live without sleep," Judy offered.

"Oh, very funny," someone mumbled.

It was Myra who brought reality home. "I think we should get some sleep. After all, there's another day and another night coming." The group agreed reluctantly, slinking off to our rooms one by one.

As I stumbled toward my bed I heard Sabra say, "I know one thing for sure: this vacation is going to be a legend."

Frontier R.N.

Umm ... the music is so pretty. I love the oboe. Oh! My eyes popped open. The music was coming from the clock radio. As I reached over to turn off the radio alarm, I thought: I'd better turn up the volume — I almost slept right through that.

The clock read 6:00 a.m. I could hear the coffee pot switch on downstairs in the kitchen. Tawny, our golden retriever, seeing that I was awake, jumped up on the bed gleefully, panting and wagging his tail. The bouncing of his big body woke Don. "Tawny, get down," he growled.

"Time to get up, kiddo," I said as I gave Don a smack on the butt.

"Okay, okay, I'm awake," he said, giving in without a struggle.

I threw on my robe and whisked away to the kids' room. "Josh, Sam, it's time to get up." Sam was up immediately. He smiled sleepily as he trotted off to the bathroom. God, that kid is good-natured, I said to myself. Josh, on the other hand, had to be dragged out of bed.

While I pulled the covers off him, a fleeting resentment passed through me. I hated the task of getting people up in the morning. Why doesn't somebody get *me* up once in a while? I asked myself. But it was an empty question, for this was one of my jobs — as the mom. "Josh, come on! I don't have time to play games. Don't forget you have to take the bus today. My car's dead, remember? I can't drive you if you miss it." I left my task, hoping it was completed and that I wouldn't have to go and drag him back out. That resentment flickered again in me.

Breakfast was the usual clumsy ordeal. Sam couldn't find his books; Josh had to change his shirt; Don was gulping down his breakfast and trying to grab a few lines from the newspaper. To avoid traffic, Don liked to leave a little early. He always rushed, even though he had plenty of time, and it made me nervous.

"Why don't you slow down? You know you've got the jump on them," I snapped.

"Just habit, I guess," he said, chuckling at himself. "I'm afraid that if I don't move fast there must be something wrong with me."

"Bye, Ma," the kids sang as they flew out the door. From the window, I watched them run to the bus stop where a dozen of their friends stood to greet them.

"Those kids have it made," I said, half to myself.

"Whaddaya mean?" Don asked from behind the paper.

"Oh, just that this is a great neighborhood for them. Lots of friends, lots of space, lots of things to play with."

"Well, that was the idea, wasn't it?" Don seemed to think that I was complaining. He had missed the envy in my voice.

"Yes, of course, it's perfect for them."

"And for you?" He had come up behind me and put his arm around my neck.

"It's nice for me too. Safe, friendly. It's very nice," I said to his nose that was now sticking in my face.

"Good!" he exclaimed. He kissed me quickly, then opened the door. As he ran out to his car he yelled, "Remember, I may be a little late tonight. We have that meeting." Don worked at a Wall Street investment firm. It was the busy season, and he often worked long hours in the spring. I never understood much about his work. He tried to explain to me what he did, but my mind just didn't seem to work that way.

"Okay, I'll keep dinner warm for you."

"Don't bother," he yelled from the driveway. "I'll grab something in the city."

"Be careful driving."

"As always," he said, smiling and waving. Soon, he too was gone and I had the house all to myself.

I washed the dishes and put everything away. Then I drew a hot bath and sank into it. It was my reward for my morning's toils. After my bath, I dressed and poured myself a cup of coffee. I sat down at the kitchen table with my housework schedule in hand.

It was Tuesday — that meant vacuuming and the upstairs bathroom in the morning, kitchen floor and the boys' room in the afternoon. I had all the housework and errands divided into daily, weekly, and monthly tasks. It was my way of getting things done without feeling overwhelmed. I despised disorganization. And in a household with three males, one had to keep on top of things or chaos quickly set in.

I pushed the schedule away and slurped my coffee. The hardest part of the day was now at hand — getting started. During this free coffee period, as I called it, I was often tempted to sit and stare out the window all day. If I let myself, I could fall into all types of daydreams and fantasies, imagining things like being single and living in the city with no kids or responsibilities. I'd have a gorgeous apartment and lots of exciting friends. Sometimes I fantasized about traveling to faraway places. I could see myself living in the Australian outback, studying something wild and fascinating. And sometimes, especially during my period, I would imagine having a wild sexual fling. I'd focus my fantasy on someone that I had seen at the store, or on the street in town, or in a theater line — always an attractive stranger.

As I sat trying to get motivated, I was aware of a dull ache that I had been getting quite often lately. It was a kind of deep sadness — or rather, an emptiness. I hated it. What was it all about? Oh well, I knew that once I got busy, it would go away.

Finally, I tore myself off the kitchen stool and ambled over to the closet to get the vacuum cleaner. Just as I was beginning my chore the phone rang. Oh good, a reprieve, I thought as I ran to answer it. "Hello?"

"Hi, Brenda? It's Joan."

"Oh, Joan — hi." I felt excited. Lately, she had been coming over to talk, and we were developing a friendship. Joan lived two houses down from ours in the complex. Just recently, before these morning visits began, she had opened up to me about herself at a neighborhood party. She told me then that she felt comfortable talking to me because I was a nurse. I hadn't worked since the boys were born, but she seemed to think I would naturally have an empathetic ear. I enjoyed this budding friendship with Joan and could certainly identify with some of the things she talked about.

"Brenda," Joan continued on the phone, "can I stop by for a few minutes? I just can't bear being in the house today."

"Uh — " I hesitated. A visit with Joan would throw off my housework schedule. Then, realizing how anal compulsive I was being I said brightly, "Yes, that'd be nice. Come on over."

I hung up the phone and put on a new pot of coffee. I found some fancy cookies in the cupboard. "Terrific!" I said, as I pulled them out and began arranging them on a plate. There was a tap at the patio door. It was Joan, waving and smiling.

"Hi, I've put coffee on," I said, letting her in.

"Great!" She plopped herself down on one of the kitchen stools.

"What's up?" I sat down across the counter from her.

Joan's eyes were a beautiful dark brown. The whites of them, I had noticed when she was excited, seemed to get bright and clear, making the brown part even darker. They were that way now.

"Nothing, really," she responded. "I just read something in a women's magazine that was very interesting.

I thought you'd be a good one to talk to about it since you're a nurse."

"About what?" I was getting intrigued.

"It's about women and orgasms — or the lack of them," she said, matter-of-factly.

I felt my face flush. "What'd the article say?" I couldn't help but be a little embarrassed, but I was also very interested.

"Well," Joan began as she fiddled with her coffee cup, "it was about how lots of women never in their lives experience an orgasm. I mean, not even by themselves. It said that many don't even know how to do it to themselves — you know, masturbate."

"Never in their lives?" I asked in amazement.

"Never!" Joan said with a solemnity that made me giggle.

"I'm sorry, I'm not laughing at the problem. It's just your facial expression."

Joan smiled, and I noticed how nicely her lips made her whole face broaden when she did that.

"I know I must seem a little serious, but the subject's kind of important to me."

I waited for her to continue. I wasn't laughing any more.

"You see, I'm like those women I was reading about," Joan confessed. She looked almost sad now. Her clear brown eyes were studying the wallpaper. "I've never had an orgasm in my life. I don't even know what one feels like. I thought I was some kind of freak until I read that article this morning. What a relief to know that it's pretty common."

"Have you ever talked to Jim about it?" I interjected.

"No," she said flatly. "What good would that do? I've always been afraid that if he knew, he would feel like he was less of a man — or think that I was less of a woman. Anyway, Jim's never been that sensitive to my needs in bed. Oh, he's not a brute or anything like that. It's just that he doesn't seem to know much about my body. He knows what he likes, so that's what we do. I really wouldn't know what to tell him to do anyway, since I don't know *how* to have an orgasm."

"And you've never masturbated?" The conversation was getting perfectly fascinating.

"No. I mean, I've tried, but I don't know what to do, exactly." She was getting a little flustered. "If I rub myself, you know, down there, it feels good, but it never goes beyond a certain pleasant turn-on. Do you know what I mean?" Her face had a pleading expression as if to say, Please don't make me keep explaining this.

"Yes, yes, I know what you mean," I said quickly. I jumped up to get us some more coffee. As I was pouring, Joan put her hand out and touched the hand that I was pouring with.

"Wait," she commanded.

"You don't want any more?" I asked.

"I brought something with me — a little relaxant." As she spoke, she pulled a bottle of Jack Daniels out of her bag. Her eyes were dancing now, the solemnity gone.

"At this time of day?" I asked, somewhat astonished.

"Oh, come on, Bren. We're talking about some pretty heavy stuff. Besides, let's have some fun." She dangled the bottle in front of me and took on a devilish expression.

"Oh, what the hell," I said with abandon. However, I couldn't stifle a little nagging concern that my housework schedule would be thrown completely out of whack.

Joan poured a healthy dose of the booze into each of our coffee cups. I added just enough coffee to be able to call it Irish Coffee. We sipped our drinks. I looked at the clock. It was 9:30 a.m. Wow, I thought. This is a new experience.

"Let's not overdo this, okay?" I said.

"Right!" she agreed emphatically. But I suspected that she wasn't being totally sincere.

We continued drinking. The liquor acted quickly and I was already a little lightheaded when Joan asked, "What about you?"

"What about me?" I said as if I didn't know what she meant.

"Do you have them — orgasms?"

"Yeah, I have them. I guess I've always been in touch with my body — pardon the pun." With the alcohol at work we both cackled uproariously. Catching my breath I continued, suddenly eager to tell all. "Even when I was little, I knew about that spot that felt good when I rubbed it. I don't know exactly when I had my first big one. But I'm sure I was very young when that pleasant turn-on led the way to — well — that *real* pleasant turn-on."

Joan was entranced. Her eyes fixed on my face as if I were telling some incredible story. She poured more whiskey into our cups. I grabbed the coffee pot and competed with her in the pouring. I knew I would have to slow down or I'd be under the table in no time.

"So, go on," Joan insisted.

"Well—" I resumed my storytelling posture. "As I got older, I did it more and more until I became real good at it." We burst into laughter again. "God, I remember, especially in high school, I did it constantly. I was so horny I thought I was going to die. By then, I was able to have as many as I wanted to — maybe even fifty at a time."

"Really?" Joan asked. Her eyes were ablaze and her mouth hung open. "You're so lucky!"

"Yeah, luck and practice." By now we were cracking up at just about everything I said. I collected myself and went on. "When I first started making love with men, though, I never had one. I couldn't figure that out. It wasn't until I was going with Don that I discovered that I could have them with a man. But only if I was in a certain position. Don was pretty good about helping me figure it out. But I do know what you mean about Jim not knowing much about your body. Don lets me experiment, but it's like he doesn't really know what turns me on, so he trusts me to determine that for myself and tell him. I guess that's okay, but sometimes I wish he'd be more interested in what makes my body tick."

"Yeah!" Joan agreed enthusiastically, curling her lips down in anger.

We sat quietly for a while, sipping thoughtfully. My head was starting to whirl. I got up to go to the bathroom and had to steady myself by holding on to the counter before I could walk. When I returned, I noticed that Joan was pouring again. I had an impulse to stop her, but then I thought, I haven't had this much fun in a long time. The hell with it! I sat back down and took a slug.

I was curious to know more about Joan, and now I was loose enough to ask. "Joan, tell me more about yourself. What is sex like for you?"

"Boring," she offered immediately. "It feels pretty good sometimes, but believe me it's nothing to write home about." We giggled. "I really don't understand why it's so important to people. You know, I was like most young people are before they have sex. I thought it was going to be this great thing. But the bottom line is that I've always wondered — is this all there is? Other people make such a big deal about it. I must be missing something. Besides the orgasm, I mean."

"You know, Joan," I interrupted, "orgasms are great and all, but I've asked myself that question too. I probably enjoy it more than you do, but I don't think sex is all it's cracked up to be either."

"But Bren, you have multiple orgasms. If you say that, then what's missing?"

After a few minutes of trying to think clearly, I said, "I really don't know."

"Bren," Joan started. She took a deep breath. "Bren—"

"What, Joan?"

"Do you think you could teach me how to have an orgasm?"

"What?"

"Could you teach me — oh, you know."

"Well, what exactly is it that you're asking? I mean, I guess I could try to offer suggestions about things you could do. Like, maybe if you rubbed the right spot — you know, your clitoris — long enough, you would have one."

"I've tried that," Joan moaned, "and nothing happens."

"Are you sure you have the right spot?"

"I'm pretty sure," she said, befuddledly. "Can you show me?" Her drunken face was open and yearning.

"Show you!" I screeched.

"Yeah," she responded weakly.

Suddenly, I was hit by the full realization of what she was asking. I sat thinking. Well, it would be from a purely clinical point of view. It wouldn't really be sexual. The poor woman is only asking for my help. She says nothing else has worked for her.

I looked over at her. She seemed almost childlike. Soft brown curls encircled her round face, caressing it. Her big eyes were looking alternately up at me and down at her hands stretched out on the counter. And the fact that she had asked for this, even though she must certainly be as frightened as me by the proposition, showed me just how badly she wanted to experience this particular kind of fulfillment. I couldn't let her down. And I had to admit that the idea excited me.

Joan was getting restless waiting for my answer. Suddenly she blurted out, "Come on, Bren, after all, you *are* a *nurse.*"

I looked at her incredulously. "This is hardly within the framework of a nurse's duties!" I said firmly.

Joan's face turned beet red, and I regretted my harshness. More softly I said, "If I do it, I'll do it as a friend — as someone who cares about you." I reached out and touched her arm. She was trembling slightly. My heart went out to her and her genuine need. We made eye contact and smiled.

Joan grabbed the whiskey bottle and poured us each another shot. "To the Big O!" she toasted. I chuckled and lifted my drink. As we clinked cups, we repeated in unison, "To the Big O." Then we chugged down the liquor.

Within seconds another wave of lightheadedness was upon me. I looked at Joan foggily. Her face wore a distorted smile. I think she's drunk, I said to myself. It crossed my mind that she might be too smashed to go through with this thing. The thought triggered a disconcerting disappointment which made me even more scared. God, I thought, I hope I'm not going to like this!

"Well, where should we go for this — lesson?" Joan asked slurringly.

I thought for a minute. "We can't go to my bedroom, that would be too weird. I know, the guest room would be perfect — lots of privacy. Let's go."

I jumped off the stool, and Joan and I made our way, clumsily, upstairs to the guest room. Once in the room we stood awkwardly for a minute, then I took the lead by pulling back the bedcovers and fluffing up the pillows. I sat down on the edge of the bed and looked at Joan. Her tiny body was reeling back and forth, and she was staring at the bed.

"I think you should take off your clothes," I instructed her gently. When she started to remove the last of her clothing, I turned away. Then my eyes drew themselves back to her body as if they had a will of their own.

She was lovely. Her breasts were quite large, her brown nipples erect. She had a slim waist, and there was just a little extra flesh on her thighs. She stood naked in front of me, waiting for my next instruction.

I was caught between wanting to get on with it and wanting to look at her some more. A keen awareness made itself known: I was enamored with her body. And the more I studied it, the more this attraction grew. Is this possible? I asked myself. It must be the booze.

She came over and lay down on the bed. My eyes followed her every move. The sight of her lying softly on the bed mesmerized me. I shook my head and tried to readjust my attitude to focus on the business at hand.

"Okay, Joan," I said with authority, "spread your legs." She spread them, slightly at first. Then, as if she were suddenly discarding all her inhibitions, she spread them wide.

An intense desire came over me. I had to touch her, to feel her flesh. Whatever mechanism I had been using to check the flow of lust was no longer operating. I reached out with a shaky hand and fondled the inside of her thigh. My whole being concentrated itself on this action, so that my trembling arm bore the brunt of my whole passion.

I ran my fingers up along the soft flesh to her labia and then back down the other leg. She let out a low moan when I swept my way back and forth over her groin. Each time my hand made this journey it lingered longer at the midpoint. Her fur became hotter and wetter each time I paused there.

Her genitals were so wonderful — so exciting — that I couldn't help but linger there with my gentle massage. I fingered the folds of skin and teased her clitoris by running my fingers around and around the erect knob.

Joan uttered noises from her gut, and her lower body swung into motion. A wetness flowed from my own cunt when she said, "Brenda, take your clothes off too." I hesitated, unable to force myself away from her long enough to comply. I was completely engrossed in slipping my fingers over her tantalizing genitalia.

Suddenly she cried out, "Oh God," and jumped up, tearing off my blouse and pulling down my bra. Then she dove at my breasts, kissing and sucking them while she pulled at my slacks. With her mouth impaled on my breast she managed to remove my clothes. A hot yearning flowed through me. Her silky lips nipping at my bosom were an irresistible turn-on. "Oh!" I yelled. "Oh, Joan, don't stop."

Now naked, I climbed on top of her, pushing her back down on the bed. I thrust my breast against her thrashing tongue and straddled her with my pelvis, clutching her. Stinging pleasure surged and bolted from my breasts to my groin and then down my legs.

A picture of her bulging hot clit blazed in my head. The memory of its lusciousness burned in my mind until I was enticed out of her suckling embrace and slid down. My fingers deftly spread her lips widely apart until she was completely exposed and purring with life. As cum dripped from her canal, I reveled in its sumptuousness, lapping and licking at it.

A fever had enveloped me, a fever of wanton desire. Never had I known such a craving. I put my mouth over her cunt and continued to dance my tongue on her. I lifted her thighs with my arms, and I left her clit to bore my way into her hole. But the sight of her stiff, throbbing clitoris continued to enthrall me, and I went back to sucking, biting, and licking it.

Joan began bouncing on the bed. She screamed out, "Oh, this is incredible! Yes — oh yes — I didn't know — don't ever stop."

I stuck two fingers into her sopping vagina, sliding in and out. I found the mushy button inside and kneaded it. She pushed her pelvis hard against my face. Her moans and gasps became quick and loud. I licked and sucked and thrust at her tirelessly, wallowing in her.

Then I stopped cold. "Oh no — don't!" Joan screamed in alarm. "Please — don't stop!" I lay there for just a moment, motionless. Then I shoved my hand up into her as far as it would go and took her clit in my mouth again, sucking so forcefully as if to almost swallow it up. Then I flattened my tongue on it, moving up and down. Joan began a crescendo of cries. Her pelvis was in a lather as I continued to press and slide, press and slide. She yanked at my hair as she screamed: "Yes — yes — *yes!*" Like a volcano her canal exploded, widening and chugging, then clamping and contracting around my fingers, spitting out cum until streams of it came rushing out of her.

I pursued my prey, unwilling to let her go. Her spasms became twitches and her body fell, like a heavy weight, onto the mattress. I kissed her thighs, her mound, her stomach. I wanted to go on and on.

Reluctantly, when I knew every possible drop of sensation had been squeezed out of her spent flesh, I pulled myself up and lay next to her. All the tension was gone. I swept the brown curls, drenched in sweat, off her forehead, and looked into her placid face. "Joan?" I called to her softly.

"Hmm?" she responded, her eyes closed, her mouth smiling.

"That was an orgasm."

The cove

I

It was my last night on the Cape. A week ago I had come alone to a quiet cottage near a marshy cove. The place was exquisitely unpeopled; only a few houses dotted the area.

The purpose of my stay was to try and come to terms with a long-abiding agony — an agony thrust upon me when I became yet one more of the countless casualties in the age-old war of man against himself. I was the victim of just another variation on the theme of self-loathing: fear and ignorance become religious fervor; and murder, righteous indignation. I had hoped that by dredging up the memories of a lifetime and the losses attached to those memories, I would somehow be able to pass through my current grief into a new beginning, and heal.

Tonight, as I walked the short distance from my cottage to the beach, I had to reckon with the reality that tomorrow, I would be leaving this place as destitute as I was when I arrived.

It had been a rainy day. Now, in the early evening, the rain had passed but clouds and fog still lingered. When I came to the small stretch of sand I immediately went over to my smooth, flat rock that nature had placed on this spot for use as a chair. There was a perfect dip in its center that I could sit in and face the water.

The night air was warm and heavy with mist. The dark, gray-black sky matched the color of the water in the bay, making it difficult to determine where water ended and sky began. The sea was very still, with only occasional tiny ripples lapping at the shore. The tide was low, and the air smelled of exposed bay floor: of slippery green silt clinging to rocks and mucky earth, of slimy sand laden with the bacteria that feeds on things living and dead; it was the scent of something decomposing. I didn't really mind the smell — it so completely coincided with my mood. And it represented to me part of the cycle of life and death, the rhythm of creation.

The place was quiet, almost completely without sound. All I could hear was a small buoy bell, the occasional slap of water, and the distant moan of a foghorn, its hollow roar warning boats away from the peninsula of rock and sand that formed the outer edge of the cove. The murky ocean air coated the area, making everything damp. Within moments of arriving on the beach, I too was covered with the sticky salt spray. Now and then a breeze came softly, filling my nostrils and mouth with the fragrance and taste of the sea.

It's remarkable, I thought as I sat absorbing the environment, how closely my surroundings parallel my condition. It's as though the cove mourns with me.

I almost had to laugh. A week ago I had come here to lighten myself of the burden of grief. Now, on my last night, it appeared as though I had only succeeded in contaminating the earth and sea around me with my gloom. "Thank you for the empathy," I said to the bay, "but I didn't come here for that. I came to heal."

II

It seemed like it was a long time ago that my life was suddenly, and perhaps permanently, changed. I had been happy once. That I did remember, though it was becoming harder and harder to remember how it felt.

More than two years had gone by since the onset of the gut-wrenching pain that now characterized my existence. But it was becoming more difficult to keep track of time passing; one day blended into another, each one the same. And it was hard to concentrate on even the most insignificant matters. How I managed to accomplish the small tasks of daily living was a mystery to me. At first, other people helped me; but after a while they grew tired of it and had gone on with their lives. How I wished that I too could go on with my life. But I was stuck — stuck in a place, a time, an event, a loss. In my mind's eye I see it happening over and over:

We're walking down a street in the Village. It's late and we're on our way home. She's holding my hand and talking — animated, excited. We hear footsteps. Someone is running up behind us. A man screams out, "Abomination unto the Lord!" With a frantic blow, he plunges a knife into my lover's back. His dagger is rammed through her heart in the name of God.

I hold her. She says nothing, but looks into my eyes with a bewildered expression. I experience a strange sensation —it's her spirit fluttering free from her body as she collapses to the ground. She falls in death gently, quietly, unmaliciously — not unlike the way she had stood in life. I kneel over her. It isn't real! But then, it is. I rise, open my throat, and bellow a loud and primitive wail of fear and despair.

He turns to run. But before he can complete his turn, his face is stopped by mine. His eyes, wide and sunken, betray a tortured soul. He says: "Evil." Then shouts, "Homosexuals must be destroyed!" He flees.

I sink back down to her and take her lifeless body in my arms. I rock her and weep and feel the world diminish.

III

Sometimes I fear that my soul went with hers that night, to that other dimension, forcing my body to stay here and go through the motions of living without the ability to feel life. At least that would explain why, after so long a time, I seemed unable to recover. I knew my grief psychology. The proper time allotted for being sanely insane had long past. Who were these egomaniacs, anyway, who believed they had the right or the wisdom to put a time limit on grief? They call it pathological grief when it goes beyond that limit. I think it's more like their pathological arrogance!

My eyes shifted from the horizon to my sneakers. Old and full of holes, they kept filling up with sand and rocks, and my feet hurt. It took me a while, these days, to notice things like that — the small irritants. Anyway, I didn't even have the energy to take my shoes off and empty out the debris. "God, I miss her," I said to my feet.

When I finally lifted my gaze back to the water's edge I saw a strange-looking bird fly across my line of vision. It wasn't a sea gull or any other seabird that I could recognize. It looked like a pigeon, except it was completely white. I turned my head to follow its flight until it disappeared into the fog. Then I caught sight of something in the corner of my eye. When I looked to see what it was I gulped a breath, startled — it was a woman! She was sitting on a rock not more than ten feet away from me.

I had to strain my eyes, in the darkness, to discern her features. Her hair was short and she wore something like a beach robe. She was leaning back on her hands and staring out at the ocean. At first I was angry at having my space invaded. How long had she been there? Did she think she was alone, as I had?

As I examined her, she suddenly turned her head in my direction. It was difficult to see her befogged face clearly, but she seemed to be smiling. My anger dropped away and was replaced by a fleeting sense of peace. I hadn't known that feeling in a while. But there it was — genuine serenity. Strangely, the fact that I was staring at the woman didn't embarrass me. I sensed a very strong draw toward her and would have said that she was luminous except there was no visible light around her.

Whatever I was sensing was coming from within her.

She turned back to the sea, then stood up. I've invaded her privacy, I thought. She's going to leave. But she didn't. Instead, she removed her garment and dropped it onto the rock she had been sitting on. She moved toward the water and I saw that she was naked. Her skin was so white that even in the fog and darkness her body was clearly visible. She stopped at the water's edge, and I examined her. Her shoulders were broad; her arms trim and toned; her legs long, taut, and sinewy. Her buttocks flared out just a bit, the muscles tight.

I thought she was going into the water, but she turned around. I could see her breasts, small and firm, her nipples pink against her white white skin. Her belly and thighs, like the rest of her, were firm. Her pubis was hairless. I did not feel uncomfortable examining her; it seemed as if she were beckoning me to look. She smiled again, turned once more, and this time went into the water. When the sea came up to her waist she twirled back around toward me and watched as if she were waiting for me.

I felt my body rise from the rock and found myself quickly and quietly removing my clothes, lastly kicking off the offending sneakers. I walked to the ocean's edge. The water lapped at my battered feet, the smooth wet sand soothing them.

My mind was void of thought, as if I were a robot following unspoken commands; my senses were clear, aware of everything. Slowly, deliberately, I moved into the warm soupy bay until I faced her. The surrounding salty liquid seemed also to be acting on command, swirling about my torso, legs, and groin. Minute fingers of syrupy water dipped into and played with my submerged cunt. Sharp sensations crawled from my sunken toes, up my legs, and around my sea-cloaked clit.

The woman took my face into her delicate hands and held it as she focused her beaming eyes into mine. The skin of her face was as white as the rest of her except for the cheeks, which had a slight pink flush. Her lips were smooth, wet, and inviting. The hair on her head was the only hair on her body. It was very black and made up of tiny curls. Her eyes were a blazing blue, like the color of the ocean when a clear sky and bright sun pierce their light into its depths. She took her hands from my face and ran her fingers through my hair. Then she gently fondled my ears, eyes, and lips, and went on to explore my body in the same exquisite manner.

When her hands made their journey to my breasts I trembled in the sensuousness of her touch. While she stroked me I became aware of another sensation — something was intricately probing my groin. It was as if she had a third hand that was tenderly milking my genitalia.

Through the sense of touch I experienced her loveliness, vividly. Her body was wondrously soft, the muscles bulging in small mounds from under her glistening skin. Her bared pubis was smooth and sweet in its baldness. Never before had I savored such a silkiness in the skin of another. While languishing in the feel of her, I made an amazing discovery. I realized that my hands hung motionless at my sides — my fingers had not touched her at all.

As I pondered this mystifying phenomenon, the woman placed her hands on my shoulders and firmly pushed me down so that I was forced to kneel in the water. My head was all that remained above the unruffled ocean pool. She moved toward me, pressing her hard white belly against my face. Then she put her arms around my head and held me. I could feel her torso expand and deflate as she breathed. Her flesh exuded a familiar scent — it was the smell of wild roses.

She slid down, her body rubbing against my face until she too knelt on the ocean floor. Then she put her mouth on mine, and although her arms were wrapped around me, I could feel something gingerly exploring my body, slithering over all of my amatory places. Subtly at first, then blatantly, I felt the sensation of lips sucking my breasts, tongues lapping at my clitoris; fingers playing in and out of my anus and vagina; mouths exploring my ears, neck, shoulders, and back; hands running over my knees, feet, and thighs. It was like a hundred hands, mouths, fingers, and lips were engaged in the act of bringing my body to its blazing liberation.

My flesh responded, becoming more and more aroused. Shivers ran the length of my spine and my body began to move urgently, unable to keep still under the onrush of rising passion. With her lips and her arms the woman held onto me tightly, compelling my flesh to be patient for the coming of its release. She was commanding me to passivity — assuring me that the onslaught of erotic satisfaction would spring forth in the fullest possible way, at exactly the right moment.

My cunt began to curdle. My throbbing breasts popped up into points. My legs trembled, every muscle palpitating. My tortured body rose and fell in the ebb and flow of flesh on the edge of its fulfillment. She clung firmly to me as I was pummeled and bedazzled by magical combinations of sensation.

Then, the flood waters came, rising and surging to their ultimate height. In a flash, my body fell into the onrushing tide as it splashed to its quintessential peak. Rivers of ecstasy rumbled through my every needy nerve. I was aglow in the release of my tumescence, airy in the relief of my despair.

IV

She continued holding me for a very long time. My head rested on her shoulder. Then she let go and I felt myself being lifted to my feet. She took my face in her hands once again and gazed at me tenderly. Tears were flowing from her bold blue eyes, streaming down her cheeks. She was crying, but somehow I knew that they were *my* tears.

Finally she smiled, kissed me softly, turned, and walked back to the shore. As I stood and watched, an invisible hand on my shoulder held me in place. I saw her bend down and write something in the sand. When she finished her sandscript she went over to the rock where she had left her robe, and put it on. Suddenly the fog rolled in so thickly that I lost sight of her. When the mist broke enough for me to see, she was gone.

In a daze I moved toward the shore. The hand I had felt on my shoulder no longer held me. She had disappeared. All was as it had been before — except that my feet no longer hurt. The bruises and blisters were healed.

I strode to my rock and put my clothes on. While dressing, I realized that something else had changed: the grief, the thing that had for so long kept my heart crushed in its viselike grip, was gone. In a moment it had left me, and with such a ferocity so as to assure me that it was gone forever.

I was filled with lightness and peace. I smiled euphorically and in jubilation, I turned to take one more look at the foggy cove. Incredibly, the clouds were breaking up, patches of stars were twinkling brightly. The misty fog seemed to vaporize into nothingness. A large round moon popped out and cast its light upon the water. Night birds sang. The water swished with gusto as the tide came in. The wind blew the scent of something sweet over me. In the moonlight I could see bushes of wild roses all around me.

Suddenly, I remembered that the woman had written something in the sand and I rushed over to that spot, hoping that the tide hadn't washed it away. A cloud passed in front of the moon, veiling its light as I began my search. Waves were coming up higher and higher on the beach. Concerned that I was running out of time, I bent down on my hands and knees to get a closer look at the ground. The light of the moon returned slowly as the cloud moved out of its way.

A few feet away from where I hovered, I saw something and scurried over to it. As I slid into the spot the moonlight threw its full glow where I knelt. I had found it! Excitedly, I tried to focus my eyes on the message. Just then a rambunctious wave came crashing in, climbing way up on the beach, over my legs and over the words in front of me. I was sure that the last bit of angelic communication would be gone, carried away by the sea.

When the wave retreated back to the bay, I beheld a miraculous thing: the words she had written were clearly there, carved neatly in the sand. Still kneeling, with my hands clasped together I read them over and over until tears of joy and gratitude flooded my vision.

"BLESSED ARE THOSE WHO MOURN, FOR THEY SHALL BE COMFORTED."

Mountain wrangler

I

Flo didn't fully realize what she was getting herself into when she signed up for the Wyoming Mountain Ride. The brochure had said that anyone considering this particular adventure should be an intermediate-level horseback rider. Flo had ridden all her life, though in the last few years she hadn't been on a horse more than a couple of times. But how good a rider can the average American be? she asked herself. She was quite sure she could handle it.

So she boarded the plane for Wyoming filled with excitement and anticipation about the seven-day journey into one of the wildest parts of the country. Flo needed an adventure, her life at home was becoming too mundane. It seemed like she knew every lesbian in the town of Portland, and she sometimes feared she'd never fall in love again. It had been a very long time since she'd met anyone who really excited her. Maybe I've had my quota of lovers for this lifetime, she thought moodily as she gazed out at the fluffy white clouds they were flying through. She chuckled at her own weird sense of logic.

Flo met the people she'd be going into the wilderness with at Fowler's Ranch, where they had all been invited for dinner that first night. This was an occasion set up by the tour owners for the purpose of bringing everyone together to meet each other and their tour guides. It was on that night that Flo got her first inkling that perhaps she wasn't as advanced a rider as she should be.

The main guide for the trip was a tall, lanky, bearded man known as the Chief. He was half Cherokee and looked to Flo like he had come right out of the Old West. He wore a broad-brimmed cowboy hat, chaps (pronounced "shaps"), and a Colt .45. His high-heeled western boots sported spurs that made a chinking noise when he walked. After dinner, the Chief stood to give the guests a little pep talk.

"I'll make this short," he began, "because I've still got some preparations to do for the trip. So listen up, please. No one knows what the weather will be in the mountains. It's completely unpredictable. Expect long hot dry days, and cold nights — possibly below freezing. It might rain for days. Thunderstorms are common. Hailstones are possible. And there can be all nature of winds. We'll be climbing up and down steep mountain trails. Once we're up on a mountain, no matter what happens, we've got to come down — can't spend the night on some mountainside. On the other hand, if it rains while we're in camp, we don't move until it stops and dries out some. We can't safely maneuver steep mountain passes if they're too muddy. So if the weather is bad for days, we're stuck in camp for days. Let's hope that will not be the case. Obviously you need to bring lots of warm clothes and good rain gear. Oh — and drink water constantly. You don't want to get altitude sickness. We'll be going up to close to thirteen thousand feet. Well, I've got to run. Hopefully we'll have good weather and a good time." He tipped his hat and started for the door. "By the way, take a good shower tonight. It'll be your last one for a while," he warned them before slipping out.

It may be my last one, period, Flo said to herself on the ride through the small cowboy town, back to the motel where they were to spend their first night. She was a bit unnerved by it all. But, after all, she had come this far. As she got into bed that night, she convinced herself that, having been athletic all her life, she'd get through this week somehow. What Flo didn't know was that no one, not even the Chief, could have prepared her for what was to come.

The next day the group was picked up by a man in a large van and rode for hours, mostly on unpaved roads, to a spot in the Shoshone National Forest. When they arrived the other guide, Valencia, was waiting for them. She explained that the Chief was running the horses down from the ranch and that when they got there one would be selected for each person based on experience and ability.

While the group of twelve stout souls awaited their mounts, they started getting to know each other. Valencia was the Chief's sister. Both of them had lived in

Wyoming their whole lives. For years, the Chief had punched cattle for a living. Then he and Valencia decided to hire themselves out to the touring business. They both knew the mountain passes like the backs of their hands.

Valencia was tall like the Chief, but carried more flesh on her bones. She was wearing a cowboy hat with pieces of decorated scrimshaw around the rim, and a cowboy shirt with the sleeves cut off, exposing her long muscular arms. She wore jeans, but no chaps. Spurs were fitted to her boots. She was a very handsome woman who smiled often, softening a tough organizer's exterior. There was a gap between her otherwise perfect white teeth. Her brownish gray hair hung in curls down her back from underneath her hat. The front and sides of her hair were cut short. She had the high cheekbones of her Cherokee heritage. When she smiled, her whole face twinkled, her brown eyes constantly sparkling. She said that the wilderness still awed her and gave her great joy. Flo believed that, because it showed when Flo caught her gazing at the mountains. From the moment Flo first placed her eyes on Valencia she knew that, if nothing else, this coming week would definitely be scenic.

Finally, a small herd of horses came rumbling down a nearby hillside toward the group. The Chief rode right up behind them. Valencia and a few others jumped up to help grab the horses before they could decide to turn and run somewhere else.

Once they got the herd settled in, the Chief assigned one to everybody. He looked each person over with a critical eye and asked, "How good a rider are you?"

Some said "expert" and the Chief seemed to believe them. Some said "expert" and he said, "Expert, huh?" and he'd give that person a horse that everyone knew was geared down a notch or two. When Flo's turn came he went over to examine her. "Well?" he said, his eyebrows raised.

Flo replied, "Maybe intermediate."

The Chief pulled at his beard. "I never quite know what that really means," he said thoughtfully.

"Okay, I'll put it this way," Flo conceded. "I haven't ridden much in the last couple of years. But I grew up riding."

"Uh-huh!" the Chief grunted. "That's a little more helpful. Do you think you can handle this Arabian? She's got a terrible lot of energy. You'll have to hold her back."

Flo mustered up her courage. "I'll give it a try, Chief."

"Atta girl!" he snorted.

While Flo was saddling her mount, Valencia came over to help. She smiled at Flo and said reassuringly, "Babe's a good horse. Just keep her in the back. She's the newest, and therefore the lowest in the pecking order. And keep a good hold on her. She's a bundle of energy and she wants to go."

"Got it!" Flo said, with more confidence than she felt. Valencia came around under the horse's head to the left side, where Flo was struggling with the cinch. She put her arm around Flo's shoulders. "I think you'll be fine," she said, giving Flo a squeeze. Flo felt her body melt. When Valencia left to assist some of the others, Flo let a smile creep over her face.

"What ya smilin' at, Flo?" the Chief asked as he passed by. The man obviously didn't miss a trick.

"Oh, just excited about everything, I guess," she responded. She glanced quickly over to where Valencia was, to see if she had caught anything. Valencia was concentrating on her task, oblivious to Flo and the Chief.

"Well, we'll see if that smile's still there when we reach the trailhead," the Chief teased. Flo refused to take him seriously. It was only a couple of hours' ride, according to Valencia. How bad could it be?

Within a matter of minutes the group was ready to go. One behind the other, the pioneers set out to conquer the wilderness. The Chief rode up front on his horse, Mr. T. Valencia moved around from place to place on her horse, Carrots, keeping watch over her flock. It was midafternoon and the sun blazed.

Soon after they had set out, they began to ascend. And shortly after that the wilderness seemed to swallow them. The views were fantastic, and oohs and ahhs could be heard as they passed over the great green gorges with clear gushing streams, surrounded by huge craggy mountains.

Flo and Babe took up the rear as instructed. Lillie, an avid horsewoman from D.C., rode in front of Flo. She turned her head and said, "Do you believe this?"

"Incredible," Flo crooned. "Valencia was right about this place."

"Uh-huh," Lillie nodded. They moved on in silence for a while, breathing in the clear, clean air and taking into their souls the vast beauty of the earth.

"I think I'm falling in love," Flo yelled out to Lill.

Lill turned her head quickly. "With who?"

"With all of it," Flo answered.

"Oh, yeah," Lillie acknowledged. "I know what you mean."

Flo had always loved the earth and sea. Its wonders never failed to give her a deep and abiding delight and respect. But never before had she experienced a place such as this. The wildflowers bloomed voluptuously. There were bright blue round ones and flaming reddish orange ones shaped like paintbrushes. Some were like white delicate doilies and some had deep purple petals. They appeared everywhere amidst the green grass and sagebrush.

The sky was bluer than she had ever seen it, the clouds whiter and fluffier. The mountains loomed around them and never-ending giant volcano spouts, long since burned out, rose into the sky. Sharp jutting peaks of rock at times looked like animal shapes or human profiles. Most, however, were just giant jagged hunks resembling immense old teeth; these were remnants of the Ice Age. And the colors of the mountains were a true wonderment, changing with the position of the sun. Sometimes they were gray, then blue, and sometimes red and orange.

The Chief kept the horses moving at a pretty fast pace, alternating walking with a fast trot. Trotting was the hard part; it seemed to Flo that nothing she did could keep her ass from being battered against the hard leather saddle. She found it particularly painful going down steep grades. The pace was too fast for the use of conventional Western riding technique to smooth the bouncing out of the ride. After about an hour of being slammed around in the saddle, Flo decided to post, English style; otherwise she'd never make it through another day — let alone a week. After a while she noticed that Lillie was posting too.

"I know you're not supposed to post when riding Western," Flo yelled to her, "but nothing else is working."

"I know, same here," Lillie acknowledged. "Look, I think this is going to be the kind of week that you do anything that helps, you know? Don't worry about doing things the right way. Just worry about getting through."

"Yeah," Flo agreed. "I don't think I'm going to have any choice."

When they had reached a summit and were riding on flatter ground just below timberline, every now and then Flo noticed a strange-looking tree. These trees looked as if they had been bombed; they were large dead stumps of varying heights. Their tops were ragged and burnt black. What was strange was that there'd be one tree like that in an area where all the other ones were normal; so Flo knew it couldn't have been from a forest fire.

They had been riding for about two hours when Valencia, who was at the back, cast a worried glance behind them. Flo followed Valencia's eyes and saw a wall of black clouds which were carrying streaks of lightning. It was then that Flo realized what had happened to those trees.

They had begun another descent when Flo felt the first few drops of rain. They rode on to a fairly level spot where the Chief stopped the group. "Okay," he instructed, "you've got five minutes to get your rain gear out and put it on. There's a storm coming up fast behind us." He gestured with his head toward the dark clouds. "We're going to be moving pretty fast to try to stay ahead of it, so everybody stay together and keep up!" By now the storm was not just behind them but was coming up on their right as well. After everyone had on their rain gear, they moved out.

The Chief wasn't kidding about moving fast. Now they were moving at a constant fast trot, and the steep downgrades were brutal on Flo's body, making her groan involuntarily from pain and exhaustion. And the race down narrow declines, twists, and turns, with nothing on one side of them but a deep rocky ravine, frightened her. The fast-approaching thunderstorm now displayed forked streaks of lightning that split the sky. Flo had read somewhere that one of the most dangerous places to be during an electrical storm was on the back of a horse because of their metal shoes. She guessed that the Chief must not have read that book.

Within half an hour the rain was coming down hard and fast, and the paths were becoming muddy. Every now and then Babe slipped, sending a bolt of pure fear shooting right through Flo's gut. She white-knuckled the reins with hands numb from the cold rain.

Just when Flo was seriously questioning her ability to get through all this alive, she thought she saw some smoke in the distance. "Lill," she shouted in desperate hope, "is that a camp up ahead?"

"Gosh," Lill shouted back after straining to see through the rain, "I think it is. Thank God, Flo — I think it is."

Sure enough, as they came off the mountain onto a flat plain, they could see a line of smoke swirling from a barely discernable hut or tent.

The horses, sensing that they were close to camp, picked up more speed, and Flo really had to work hard at holding Babe back. The end in sight gave the riders a boost of strength, just enough to enable them to survive the last bit of their ride that day. They hooted and hollered as they came tromping into the camp at a fast lope, soaked to the gills, exhausted to the bone, and with lightning licking at their heels. As they worked feverishly to unsaddle their horses, the storm hit fully.

The dripping duo of Flo and Lill limped over to the campfire to warm up. A sheet of canvas was staked above the fire to keep the rain off. A big pot of stew was cooking along with fry bread and coffee. There was a large white tent nearby and even a makeshift outhouse, which was actually more of an out-tent.

As Flo warmed her bruised bottom and unwound her fear-wrenched gut, she said to Lill, "I think my ovaries have dropped into my uterus."

"Hell," Lill chuckled, "I lost mine a long time ago, back there on the trail." They burst out laughing, giddy from exhaustion and grateful to be off their horses.

Valencia came over to the fire and announced, "The tents are all set up; better put a claim on yours now. And grab a sleeping bag on your way — they're over there under the tarp."

Flo picked up her saddlebags, selected a sleeping bag, and chose a tent not too far from the campfire, where she figured she'd be spending a lot of time hanging out that night. Squeezing into the two-person tent, she changed into dry clothes, then went back to join the group. By now the rain had stopped and dinner was being served. Flo found the stew and fry bread most delicious, and the warm fire felt truly wonderful to her.

After dinner they all relaxed, sipping coffee and hot cocoa around the campfire. Lorin and Stacey, the couple hired to set up the camp and do the cooking, pulled out their guitars and began singing. As the sun was setting, some of the guests took short hikes to view the magnificent multicolored sky. Hues of pink, red, and orange changed to lavender, purple, and dark blue as the stars came out, twinkling large and bright in the clear high mountain atmosphere.

One by one the pioneers slipped off to their tents. Though her body was rejuvenated by the food and warmth, Flo's eyelids soon grew heavy and she too bid her good nights and headed for the makeshift outhouse, and then her tent.

She was fast asleep, toasty warm in her sleeping bag, when she heard a loud thud against the side of her tent. She awoke fully, frightened by the possibilities of what could be out there pawing at her tent.

Then a voice said, "Flo — Flo, it's me, Valencia. Can I come in?" Flo jumped up and unzipped the tent flap.

"Sure, come on in," she answered, excited and curious. Valencia crawled inside. In the glow of the flashlight she carried, Flo saw that she had a sleeping bag with her.

"Did I wake you?"

"Yeah, but that's okay," Flo assured her. "It's nice to have company — especially you."

"Thanks," Valencia said, captivating Flo with her smile. "The Chief is snoring and he's keeping me awake. Besides, he's not much fun to sleep with. Would it bother you if I slept here?"

"Not at all. Set your bag right here." Flo patted the tent floor next to her.

Valencia unrolled and opened her bag, then glanced at Flo self-consciously. "Uh ... you know these bags zip together to make a double. If we did that we'd be warmer," Valencia offered tentatively.

"I'll say," Flo blurted out, and they giggled. "Let's do it," Flo said, desperately trying to remain calm.

She slipped out of her bag and they zipped the two together. Then they slid inside and lay on their backs. Valencia turned off the flashlight. In the darkness of the small tent Flo could feel the warmth of Valencia's robust body. As she listened to her breathing, her own body started to tingle. Suddenly she felt Valencia's body shaking, and soon she heard chuckling. Then Valencia was laughing boisterously.

"What are you laughing at?" Flo asked, wanting in on the fun.

Valencia tried to talk but could only splutter.

"What?" Flo asked again.

Valencia finally said, in spurts, "You — you were so funny today. Espe-especially when you and Lillie started mo-moaning every time we trotted down a hill. And your face!" She howled. "When that storm hit, your face turned stone white. You looked like one of the mountain rocks. We should've left you there as our own version of Mount Rushmore."

Flo giggled too as she pictured how she must have looked, and soon they were both laughing riotously. Flo told Valencia about what Lill had said about her ovaries, and Valencia roared some more.

"But—" Valencia spit out amidst the fits of laughter. She turned to lie on her side facing Flo, and Flo turned toward her.

"But what?" Flo asked, still chuckling.

"But you did a fantastic job with Babe. She's a tough horse to handle and you did it. A lesser rider would have lost control of that Arabian." She was smiling, but had stopped laughing.

Flo studied her to see if she was teasing. When she was convinced that Valencia was serious she said, "God — thanks!" Flo was amazed that anyone could compliment her riding skills.

When all the laughter had ceased they found themselves gazing quietly at each other. Then Valencia pulled her hand out of the sleeping bag and touched Flo's face. She leaned forward and kissed her lightly, barely touching Flo's full, sensual lips. Though the kiss was delicate, it had an urgency that was soon resolved when Flo responded by moving toward Valencia. They brought their mouths together fully, abandoning all reservation. Flo reached her arm around Valencia's neck with a forceful summons, and Valencia whimpered as she moved on top of Flo. She gently brushed back Flo's wavy black hair and softly ran her mouth all over her round, dimpled face. Then as she took Flo's face between her hands, she played her lips on Flo's, alternating tender glides with quick jabs. Flo's body became a slave to the luring commands of Valencia's lips, and small shivers spread from her mouth to the back of her neck and down her spine.

As she felt sudden bursts of tremors in Valencia's body, Flo too shook in her own volatility from the expert engaging of Valencia's mouth, and the passion that was rising in them both. Flo tried to keep still in order to feel the wonderful arousal of her lover's lust. But lying under this large vibrant woman who smelled of campfire and the outdoors was more than she could take, and she could not hold back her own body's charged-up twitching and quivering.

Valencia rose up and looked into Flo's eyes for a moment. Then, straddling Flo's torso, she slowly removed the sweatsuit that Flo had worn to bed. She unzipped the hooded sweatshirt as if she were peeling a piece of luscious and delicate fruit, spreading it open and taking it off one sleeve at a time. She then edged Flo's t-shirt up over her breasts, laying them bare. Flo could hear Valencia's breathing become heavier as her legs clutched Flo's pelvis and her groin heaved into tremors again. She sucked in air and held tightly onto Flo until the trembling stopped.

Lightly running her fingers over Flo's breasts, Valencia whispered breathily, "Oh, Flo, your breasts are so beautiful." She cupped them in her hands and moved them around in a circular motion, Flo's erect nipples tickling her palms and sending charges of sensation streaking up her arms. Her legs and pelvis shook again, more powerfully, and now her hands and arms vibrated along with the rest of her. Another whimper came from Valencia as fluid slid out of her cunt in a gush.

Valencia's massaging of Flo's sensitive nipples, along with her own visible stimulation, aroused Flo at her very center so that the muscles in her belly jerked and twitched. Her cunt pulsated hot and wet. She raised her hands to grab onto Valencia, but before she could capture her Valencia moved down, straddling Flo's ankles. With one smooth and delicate motion, she pulled Flo's sweatpants and panties down her legs and off. Then she quickly flung off her own clothes and slid back on top of Flo, their naked bodies now quaking together with desire, flesh on flesh.

Valencia nibbled at Flo's ear, playing her tongue around the opening, occasionally plunging it into the canal. Flo finally was able to catch hold of Valencia's steaming body. She languished in the flesh of her buttocks and back. Valencia's expert tonguing was a tremendous turn-on, and Flo was amazed at how this woman seemed to know about the ultrasensitivity of her ears. Her body floated in a pool of pure passion as her cunt craved for release, gyrating under Valencia. Valencia's hot, uneven breaths whispered loudly in her ears, and Flo cried out to be plundered. "Valencia," she pleaded, "fuck me." She pressed her pelvis hard against Valencia's belly, trying desperately to rub her demanding, explosive clit on some small part of her lover's body.

Valencia had brought Flo to exactly where she wanted her, but she too had come to the threshold of a consuming desire that threatened to free itself in a wild, uncontrollable display. Flo screamed out again, "Valencia, please!" as she writhed, trapped under the control of her magnificent lover, the pressure in her groin mounting.

Then Valencia gave in to her own unbridled lust and slithered downward, pausing momentarily to suckle Flo's breasts. "Oh God," Flo cried in desperation. "Now — *now*!" Her body shook wildly from the trauma of erotic need, and Valencia made her way down to Flo's wanting, pounding crotch. Spreading her labia wide with her hands, she attacked Flo's burning clit with her hard, flat tongue. She flogged and sucked it as Flo's pelvis bounced against her. Then Valencia slipped her long fingers into Flo's soaked, contracting vagina and pressed them up against her G-spot, thrusting back and forth harder and harder, deeper and deeper. Flo's cum flowed out in rivers and she groaned, her gut clenching with the rising pleasure. Valencia kept Flo on the ultimate brink until finally, Flo wailed in delight at the release of her ecstatic agony as her body flounced and flew in a gale of erotic pleasure.

Valencia's body twitched and trembled again in the afterglow of their sparkling union; then they lay motionless. Flo, spent beyond satisfaction, tried to lift her heavy body. But Valencia gently pushed her back down and lay next to her.

"But I want to make love to you," Flo protested weakly.

"My love," Valencia said quietly, "you already have. I've been coming from the very beginning. I don't think there's anything left."

Flo's mind became suddenly alert. "You mean, you've been having one immense orgasm since we started?" she asked, astonished.

"Not quite," Valencia answered, chuckling softly. "More like a bunch of them, one right after another."

Flo looked at her. Valencia just nodded and smiled.

"Wow!" Flo said in awe. "Does that happen to you all the time?"

Valencia said seriously, "It's never happened before." Then she raised her head and looked down at Flo with a glow of love in her eyes. At that moment, they both knew this was the beginning of something much more significant than a one-night stand.

With arms and legs entangled, they fell asleep. They had been sleeping heavily, their exhausted bodies in serious recovery, when a male voice awakened them: "If you're gonna stay in there all night, then you're taking this beast with you." The tent zipper was suddenly jerked up and a lumpy, furry object was placed inside.

"What's that?" Flo asked in alarm.

"Oh, that's just Aussie. The Chief brought him over."

"How did he know you were here, and who's Aussie?" Flo inquired, confused.

As if in answer to her query, a black-and-white ball of fur stumbled over the sleeping bags up toward the women's heads. "A puppy!" Flo squealed. They both sat up at once and Aussie wagged his tail. "Where'd he come from?"

"One of the cowboys from a ranch near here brought him out tonight. The Chief gave him to me for a birthday present. He's part cow dog, and we think part Australian shepherd. They're bred to work with cattle."

Valencia picked him up lovingly and rubbed her nose against his snout. He began licking her face all over. "He's so sweet!" Flo said as Valencia handed him to her. He took to Flo as if he had known her all of his two months of life. "Friendly, aren't you!" Flo said to him. He licked her too.

Valencia made a sleeping place for him down by their feet. They lay back down to go to sleep, then Flo remembered her question. "Valencia," she asked, "how did the Chief—"

"He doesn't miss a thing," she interrupted. "It's uncanny. I think he just watches people a lot and figures things out that way."

"And he doesn't mind ... uh ... about you being with women?"

"He's used to it, I guess. Anyway, he's never said anything. He believes in letting people live their own lives. Hey, he's no angel ya know. Women are always going goofy over him on these trips. He does very well for himself."

"Yeah," Flo said nonchalantly, "I can see why."

"Watch it, Flo baby — you're mine!" Valencia laughed.

"Oh, I didn't mean for me," Flo said, flustered. Valencia just kept laughing and threw an arm around her. Within moments they were sleeping peacefully.

II

When Flo awoke in the morning, Valencia and Aussie were gone. Hearing voices out by the campfire, she unzipped the tent flap and flipped it back. Warm sunshine flowed in, and beautiful blue sky greeted her. She dressed hurriedly and hustled out to join the others.

Breakfast was being served. Valencia sat playing with Aussie, eating and talking. As Flo took her plate of pancakes and bacon over to a tree stump and sat, she caught Valencia's eye. Valencia winked, and Flo tried unsuccessfully to stifle a smile.

When everyone had eaten, washed up, and packed their gear, the Chief called them together for the day's instructions. "When you've finished tacking up your horses, I'll come and tighten the cinches. We'll be doing a lot of climbing today, so drink plenty of water. We're going up above timberline, about thirteen thousand feet. And let's move. Time's a-wasting."

Soon they were back in the saddle, trotting in single file. The Chief had Aussie in a canvas sack hooked to his saddle horn. All that could be seen of the dog was his little head sticking out.

After about an hour of ascending and descending, the group began a long uphill climb. Some of the way was very steep, and everyone was instructed to lean forward in the saddle to reduce the stress on the horses.

Whenever they came to a fairly flat area, one particular group member would behave in a dangerous and obnoxious manner. Gabrielle, a young woman with more nerve than brains, kept badgering the Chief about cantering and galloping. The trip was too slow for her. The fact that these mountain passes were not the right places to safely move at that kind of speed didn't seem to faze her, and the Chief told her flatly that if she wanted to gallop she was on the wrong ride. But she wouldn't give it up. She'd get out of line and ride to the back, just behind Babe and Flo. Then she'd kick her horse hard and make a short gallop to the front.

The first time the Chief caught her doing this, he

became very annoyed. "You're gonna spook the other horses doing that. Don't do it!" he ordered.

She quit for a while, but when she thought he couldn't see her she started up again. Babe was agitated by her horse's sudden movements, and Flo had a hard time keeping her from taking off after Gabrielle's horse. One time, Gabrielle came so close to Babe that her horse kicked Babe hard, missing Flo's leg by inches. At that point Flo yelled, "Get back in line!"

The others were fed up too by then and they echoed Flo's anger. "Yeah," someone said, "you're asking for trouble. Someone's going to get hurt." But despite the unpopularity of this little trick of hers, Gabrielle wouldn't stop. At lunchtime, Flo saw the Chief and Valencia speak to Gabrielle and guessed that they were reprimanding her.

The place where they had stopped for lunch was a large, beautiful meadow. The Wind River, or one of its tributaries, wound around the grassy space, and tall trees lined the riverbank. The horses rested, drinking and grazing. The guests sat in small groups eating, talking, and basking in the hot, dry Wyoming sun. Flo hung out with Lillie and Joanna.

"How'd y'all sleep last night?" Lillie asked.

"Fine," Joanna said immediately. "I could sleep outside all the time. I love it."

Joanna, an expert horsewoman, had been on a number of these trips and almost qualified as another guide. She could be depended upon to help the other riders not as knowledgeable as herself whenever possible. Also, the Chief trusted her. And when the Chief trusted someone, that person deserved it. Flo had already appreciated Joanna's help more than once.

"How about you, Flo?" Lill asked. "Did you sleep?"

"Oh, I had no problem sleeping," Flo assured her.

"Good," Lillie said. After they finished their lunches of sandwiches and fruit, Flo lay on her back and gazed up into the high branches of a tree. A redtail hawk circled and wound in and out of her line of vision, and her mind drifted back to the night before. A tingling, yearning sensation welled up in her. She recognized the feeling and knew that if it stayed with her, she was going to have a tough time leaving Wyoming at the end of the week.

When this realization fully hit, she sat up abruptly. Looking around, she spotted Valencia lying about twenty feet away, her muscled arms stretched out to the sides. She had on an aquamarine cowboy shirt with the sleeves cut out, as was her style. Her hat was pulled down over her face, and her curly hair was spread out on the grass in disarray. The sun shone on her exquisite frame, and as Flo watched her lying there, that feeling clutched at her insides again. "Oh, God," she mumbled.

Flo's sudden movement had caught Lillie's attention, and now Lillie was watching her curiously. She followed Flo's gaze to Valencia and then back, catching her expression. Lillie was quite aware of what she was seeing. "Well, I'll be damned!" she said to herself.

That afternoon, as promised, they made it to the top of a mountain thirteen thousand feet up. Stopping to take in the fantastic views, they saw a herd of elk loping along across a nearby mountaintop. Then a cloud passed over, and for a few minutes it dropped marble-sized hailstones on the group. When it passed, the sky was utterly clear again.

They headed down off the mountain and the steep, twisting descent left Flo's butt and legs quite sore by the end of the day. Whenever they trotted she moaned, pleading silently for camp. Finally, they met up with the packhorses and the Chief told them to set up camp. "Thank you!" Flo said loudly.

Lillie laughed and said, "Amen!"

After dinner that night, Flo went for a walk. The sun had long since set, leaving behind a dark blue sky with stars looking almost close enough to touch. The luminous glow from the full moon provided plenty of light. Flo strolled over a hill to a patch of fir trees. A thick layer of pine needles covered the ground, making the area spongy, soft, and dry. She sat, letting her spirit run free in the forest. She inhaled deeply, cleansing her lungs with the mountain air. Breathing out with a long sigh, she leaned back on the pine needles with her hands.

Suddenly something grabbed at and nibbled on one of her hands. She yanked her hand away and was about to jump up when she saw that it was a black-and-white furry puppy. "Oh, Aussie," she said, her heart still pounding. She turned and saw Valencia on her knees, laughing and holding her stomach.

Flo got to her feet, ran over, and tackled her. "You think that's so funny," she yelled in mock seriousness. "I almost had a heart attack." Soon they were both rolling around in the grass, laughing. Eventually they wandered over to the patch of pine needles under the trees and made love in the moonlight.

Later, Valencia sat up and pulled something out of her pocket. "Here, this is for you," she said, handing it to Flo. "I found it in the river today when we stopped for lunch."

Flo held it out and saw that it was a blue-green rock that had been sculpted perfectly round and smooth by the constant, powerful rush of the waters.

"It's beautiful!" Flo said, caressing it with her fingers.

"I thought you'd like it," Valencia said, smiling.

"I love it!" Flo exclaimed as she pulled Valencia close and kissed her softly.

Meanwhile, back at the campfire everyone was sitting and listening intently to the Chief telling a story: "This guy Earl and me went up on the mountain one afternoon to run some horses down to the ranch." The campfire lit up the Chief's face, and his hat was pushed back on his head. He pulled at his straggly, gray-brown beard as he went on with his story.

"And Earl, see, he had this thing about antlers. No matter how small it was — if he saw an antler on the ground, he'd pick it up. And he was riding this horse that I thought was sorta goofy anyway. Now, when you run horses, you're *runnin'* horses — I mean, you're really moving. You've got to keep up with them or you'll lose 'em. They'll take off in another direction. And there's Earl, with both hands full of antlers and trying to hold the reins.

"There was this river we had to run these horses through. Well, the horses that we're runnin' get to the river and just plain stop cold. I saw what they were doing so I pulled up on my horse and stopped next to them. I could see Earl coming down behind me on the other side of the horses. He's flying like there's no tomorrow, completely oblivious of the situation at hand. And I'm sitting there wondering what this fool, with those antlers in his hands, is going to do. He's galloping off the mountain towards the river.

"Now, the bank of this river is about four feet high. And here comes Earl and his horse, runnin' right on over the edge into the river and *bam*! the horse slams his chest right into the riverbank. Earl flies off the horse, is sailing in the air with his arms stretched out and his hands still gripping those antlers." The Chief stood up and held out his arms to demonstrate.

"Well, he landed in the trees with a crash, and I ran over. Everything was stone quiet for a minute, and I thought he must be dead. Then there he comes stumblin' out of the trees, unhurt, without even a scratch on him. And damn if he didn't still have those antlers clasped in his hands. He hadn't lost a one."

Val and Flo came up on the group just as the Chief was finishing his story. Everyone was laughing, and the Chief was quite pleased with himself. "What's going on?" Flo asked.

"Oh, you just missed a great story," Lillie said.

"I did? Damn!" Flo said, trying to sound disappointed.

The Chief looked hard at Flo and Valencia. "Yep, you two just missed one of my famous stories," he said to them, shaking his head. Flo was embarrassed, but Valencia just stared at him with a look that said: I know what you're up to. Just when Flo started to squirm, he let her off the hook. "Don't worry, I've got plenty more," he said lightheartedly.

Valencia nudged Flo with her elbow and winked. "He likes you," she whispered. Then they joined the group around the fire.

They had camped rather high up that night, and the next day they did a lot more downhill climbing. It was, as far as Flo was concerned, the most dangerous trail they had been on up to now. There were many steep, twisting declines culminating into very steep brief ascents, which the horses actually had to hop over. There were fewer level places and the gorges were deeper. Also, the paths were extremely narrow — one false move and it would be all over. By now Flo had come to trust Babe's surefootedness, which greatly helped to assuage her fears.

Gabrielle wasn't fazed by any of it. Flo thought that perhaps she was brain-damaged, and Lill agreed with her. Either that, they decided, or maybe she just had no fear. Whenever there was even the slightest bit of flat earth on either side of the group, Gabrielle would romp. Neither the Chief nor Valencia seemed to notice this.

"You know, what she's doing could really get somebody hurt," Lill said.

"I know," Flo acknowledged. "Think we should tell Valencia and the Chief?"

"They've already talked to her once. What more can they do?" Lill mumbled angrily. "She's impossible."

"I think I'll say something to Valencia at lunch," Flo decided. "I'm really concerned about the danger, especially on this trail."

"Yeah, all right. I'll go with you," Lill agreed.

As the day progressed the party got split up a bit, and some people were lagging way behind. Terry and her boyfriend Mark had stopped to look at something, so they and a few others who were behind them got separated from those in the lead. Flo moved up front for a change. They were moving along at a pretty good clip when Flo saw Valencia ride up and talk to the Chief, then turn and head back. As she rode past Flo she said, "I'm going back and get the rest of the group to catch up. Gabrielle is back there with them, and anyway it's not good to get separated like this." Then she was off.

The Chief led Flo and the others ahead a short distance until they came to a wide, flat field. They stopped there to wait for Valencia to bring the others up. The horses scattered to graze and the riders relaxed, some dismounting to stretch their legs. Flo took her feet out of the stirrups to relax her knees.

About five minutes went by. Joanna was looking back at the trail, watching for the arrival of the stragglers. Flo glanced over at her and saw an expression of horror cross Joanna's face. Before she could turn and see what the trouble was, she saw the Chief gallop up to Joanna and hand her the sack with Aussie in it. Then, he turned Mr. T. sharply back toward the woods and sprang into a gallop. When Flo looked she saw Carrots, Valencia's horse, coming out of the woods — without Valencia.

Her heart dropped to her stomach and her brain whirled. She automatically put her feet in the stirrups and was pulling Babe around when Joanna said, "Everybody stay here. Let the Chief handle this. You'll only get in the way if you go. If he needs any of us, we'll know soon enough."

As hard as it was to stay put, Flo knew Joanna was right. She relented, and waited in fear. She hadn't liked the way the Chief looked when he took off. And she knew he didn't panic easily.

The other riders were speculating aloud about what they thought might have happened. But Flo couldn't talk. As the minutes dragged by, she became more and more agitated. She kept seeing pictures in her mind of the treacherous trail they had just come over and those bottomless drops. "God, please let her be all right," she prayed. I've never loved anyone so much, she said to herself.

Finally she saw Mark riding out of the woods, pulling Terry's horse behind him. As Flo strained her eyes, she thought she could see two more people on foot, and moved Babe forward to get a better look. She was right — it was Valencia, walking with her arm around Terry, who was crying. "Oh, thank God," Flo said out loud. Then, behind the two women, the others slowly came riding out of the woods into the meadow. Taking up the rear was the Chief, looking very angry, and Gabrielle looking very sheepish.

Valencia helped Terry back on her horse, then climbed up onto Carrots. She trotted immediately over to Flo, whose face hadn't yet regained its full color and whose hands were visibly trembling. Valencia looked at her and grinned.

"What'd ya think — that I went over the edge?"

Flo stuttered when she tried to talk. "I didn't know — what — I was terrified." Valencia stopped smiling and gazed at her with the same loving expression Flo had seen on her face that first night in the tent. "You're not going to get rid of me that easily, Flo baby." Then she said abruptly, "It was that asshole Gabrielle. I'll tell you about it later."

That night in the tent, Valencia explained to Flo what had happened. "Terry and Mark were lagging behind with a few others who had stopped to watch a family of moose drinking out of the river. I got them all back on their way, and we were moving along pretty fast even through some of those tricky parts of the trail. I felt it was important not to stay separated from the rest of the group too long. As we trotted through this particular part of the trail — you know, where it opens up a little and flattens out for a couple of hundred feet..."

"Yeah, I remember that." Flo said, nodding.

"Well, I was in front setting the pace. And Gabrielle, figuring I wouldn't see her, pulled her horse out of line and held him back, like she's been doing, so she could canter across that flat spot. Terry and her horse Tequila were in the back. When Gabrielle spurred her horse, Tequila got spooked. He reared and bucked, and Terry fell off of him right into the ravine. I heard a scream and when I snapped my head around, I saw Terry going over the edge. For all I knew she could've been falling a thousand feet down. I galloped over and jumped off Carrots, half expecting to see her spread across the rocks at the bottom of the ravine. But luckily — and I mean by pure luck — she had fallen just a few feet down into some bushes that were growing out of the side of the mountain. I grabbed a rope from my saddle and tied it to myself. Mark and the others held the other end while I went down to get Terry. I checked to make sure she was okay, then we climbed up the twenty feet or so back to the trail.

"Terry was pretty scared. She couldn't stop crying, and was too upset to get back on her horse, so I smacked Carrots on the rump and yelled at her to go. I knew she'd meet up with the rest of you and in that way signal the Chief that we had run into trouble. Then we started walking back." Valencia paused and ran her hands through her hair. "It was really a close call," she said quietly.

"When the Chief got there, I told him what had happened, and he gave Gabrielle hell. He told her that for the rest of the trip she was to ride right behind him. And he said he hoped she wasn't planning on ever riding on one of these trips again."

"Whew!" Flo whistled. "Thank God Terry didn't get killed."

"Yeah," Valencia said somberly. "I don't have the words to tell you how I felt when I saw her going over the edge."

Flo held Valencia for a long time that night — partly because she was so relieved that she hadn't lost her, partly because she could feel the fear that Valencia was struggling with deep inside, and partly, simply because it felt so good.

The next morning when Flo awoke, Valencia and Aussie were long gone, as usual. When she sat up, yawning and stretching, she spotted a pile of little flowers lying next to her sleeping bag. She picked one up and examined it. Each purple petal looked like the tiny head of an elephant. There was a brief note next to the flowers that read: "They're called elephant flowers. Love, Valencia."

Once again, Valencia knew instinctively the kind of thing that would fascinate Flo. A smile crept over her mouth and the now familiar hot, yearning sensation filled her again. "This is serious stuff," she said aloud as she dropped the little flower back on top of the others. She got dressed in a daze.

When Flo finally got herself together and flipped open her tent door to get out, her eyes took in an amazing sight. The night before, they had pitched their tent on the edge of a grassy plain overlooking a section of the raging Wind River. The river was about twenty feet wide here, and deep enough in some places to actually bathe in. When Flo's eyes had adjusted to the bright sunlight, she saw the Chief stumbling across the river carrying his boots, wearing his cowboy hat and nothing else. Evidently the stones at the bottom were hurting his feet, because he was yelping out obscenities and his lean body was hunched over. Flo guessed that he had bathed and now, wet and cold, was trying to get back to his clothes as fast as he could. Flo found it a most hilarious thing to behold.

Flo bounced out of the tent and stood up. Her tent site towered about thirty feet above the river. She walked over to a clearing where she knew the Chief would be able to see her and yelled, "Hey Chief, need any help?"

He looked up at her, quickly covered his genitals with the boots, and said, "Shit!"

When the other campers heard Flo yelling they hustled over to see what was up. Soon the whole group was watching the Chief slip and slide in his rush across the river, and they burst into laughter. Some rushed to get their cameras. Finally, in exasperation, the Chief stopped midstream. He stood up straight, faced the crowd, and yelled: "Okay, you perverts, here it is! Get an eyeful!" He dropped his boots to expose himself, then he turned around and around with his hands clasped together over his head like a ballerina. Everyone howled in glee. A couple of the women shrieked. One of the men whistled.

Then the Chief waved his hand in dismissal and continued his journey. "Well, we've just created another story for him," Valencia chuckled as they watched him hobble away.

III

The last day of the trip was a five-hour ride back to the trailhead, and Flo spent most of that morning just thinking. She couldn't bear the idea of the trip ending, hopping on a plane home, and never seeing Valencia again. Even though they had known each other for only a week, the circumstances and the place had brought them closer together much more quickly than it would have happened in normal life. She felt as if she had known Valencia all of her life.

Valencia too was uncharacteristically quiet that day. Every now and then she'd drop back and ride silently alongside or behind Flo. Lill would catch them looking at each other with sadness and love. Lill had figured the whole thing out long ago.

At lunch that day, Lill pulled Flo aside. "I know it's none of my business, Flo, but a person would have to be blind, deaf, and dumb not to be able to see what's going on between you and Valencia."

Flo looked shocked. Then, her face mellowed as the realization hit her that it really didn't matter who knew. She had something else to worry about. "I'm glad you brought it up," she said. "I do need to talk to somebody. I just don't know what to do or if there is anything I can do. I feel wretched."

"Yeah," Lill nodded understandingly. "I imagine the thought of leaving here must be tearing you up."

"I guess I could come back in a couple of months for another week." Flo was desperately grasping at straws. "But how am I going to live through a couple of months without her? And then to see her for only another week?" Flo shook her head. "This is terrible. I mean, it's wonderful but it's terrible."

"Let's keep thinking," Lill suggested positively. "Maybe we can come up with some sort of plan."

"Yeah, maybe," Flo said. She felt slightly better, believing that possibly something could be worked out.

As they were mounting their horses after lunch, Valencia rode up to Flo and held her back, letting the others move out ahead of them. "Flo, you can't go home," she said bluntly. "I've been thinking. You can stay here. You can move in with me and the Chief until you and I can get our own place." Her face was earnest as she pleaded her case. "The Chief won't mind you staying. He likes you. And Flo," she paused, waiting for Flo to look up at her, "I love you."

"I love you, too!" Flo said, as tears welled up in her eyes. "But I can't just stay. What about my job, my life at home?"

"Well, I know one thing," Valencia said sadly, "my life isn't going to be much fun now without you."

"Oh God! What did we do to ourselves?" Flo cried.

"We fell in love!" Valencia said simply. "And I don't know about you, but for me this is a rare condition. Oh sure, I've fooled around a lot, especially on these trips when you know you don't have to see the person after the week is over. But I knew right away that it was going to be different with you."

"Yeah," Flo sighed, "I thought that it was just going to be a week-long fling when I first realized there was a mutual attraction. But I also knew the moment I laid eyes on you that you were special. Real special!"

They rode on in silence for a while. "Look," Valencia said finally, "as we get closer to the trailhead, things are going to start moving really fast. The horses know the trailhead well and they'll be hot to get there where the hay is waiting. We won't have much of a chance to talk because I'll have to be on my toes. Please, I beg you — think about staying?"

"Okay," Flo said, "I'll think."

Flo didn't want to tell Valencia what she was thinking, that the proposition was really not possible. How could she just stay? She had friends, family, and work waiting for her back home — two thousand miles away. To drop her whole life back there for a woman she had known for only a week would be crazy. Even if she had never in her life felt about anyone the way she felt about this woman. Even if she may never feel like this about anyone again. Even if this place was the most beautiful and fascinating wilderness she had ever seen. Still — how could she just stay?

As usual, Valencia was right. Toward the end of the trip everything speeded up. The horses, eager to get to the trailhead, were cantering instead of trotting and trotting instead of walking. When they made it to the camp, trucks, vans, and people were waiting. Tour people hustled everyone off the horses so they could run them back to the ranch and bring down fresh ones for another group that was waiting.

Flo barely had time to see Valencia before she was ushered into the big van to be shuttled back to her motel in town. Just before the van sped off, Valencia managed to slip a piece of paper through the window to Flo. On the paper the message read: STAY — call me 837-4200 — I Love You! Flo tucked the note into her pocket and rode the several hours back to town in silence while the others gabbed. She looked out at the views of mountains, winding streams, sagebrush, wildflowers, and aspen trees; and the moving scenery of antelope, cattle, horses, deer, and hawks.

When they reached the motel the driver, Bill, said, "I'll be back to pick y'all up for the good-bye dinner at Fowler's Ranch at six o'clock tonight. Okay, everybody?"

"Right!" they acknowledged. Flo said nothing but gathered up her gear and trudged off to her room. She took a long hot shower and then puttered around the room in her underwear. She had decided not to go to the ranch for dinner. She didn't want to see Valencia — to have to tell her the awful truth. She lay down on the large bed and cried until she fell asleep from utter exhaustion.

She was dreaming of cliffs and kisses when she was awakened by a knock at the door. Suspecting who it was, she didn't bother to get dressed. When she eased the door open, there stood Valencia. She had on a bright orange cowboy shirt with the sleeves cut off, and a sleeveless blue denim vest. Her hair hung in freshly washed curls out from under her cowboy hat, pulled down low on her forehead. A large silver belt buckle glimmered above her tight, well-worn jeans. Her cowboy boots were fancy and clean. She wore her bandanna like a bandit — loose around her neck. Her skin was even a deeper tone of brown from the blazing sun of their last day's ride.

Her face was serious. "Come on in," Flo said. For a moment Valencia just stood and stared at her. Then she took a few steps into the room and shut the door behind her. She brought her body up against Flo's, and Flo could feel her muscles pulsating with tension. She caressed Flo's face softly with her fingers, then kissed her deeply and tenderly.

Flo's blood surged through her, hot and fast. Valencia slid her thigh in between Flo's legs and pressed firmly on her cunt. Flo clutched at Valencia's tight butt, pulling her closer while rubbing herself against Valencia's hard thigh. Valencia ran her fingers under Flo's panties, kneading her ass as she continued to move against Flo's throbbing groin. She slipped Flo's panties down, and Flo was riding naked on the sinewy muscles of her lover's leg.

Valencia then quickly removed Flo's bra. With Flo completely naked, Valencia pulled her close and held her in a tight embrace. Valencia's body shook violently, as if a chill had suddenly grabbed her belly and trickled up her spine and down her legs. Flo now knew well what those sudden, quiet tremors of Valencia's body were. The excitement of her lover's orgasm stirred Flo's tingling body into a fervor, and she flung herself upon Valencia's rhythmically gliding thigh. Valencia ground her limb hard against Flo's cunt.

An aching desire reared and bucked in Flo as she galloped toward the precipice of her fulfillment. "Oh, Valencia," she cried, "I love you!" As Flo hung on the teetering edge of her release all movement stopped. Valencia had grasped her and was holding her with a frantic strength as another burst of violent tremors overtook her. The force of Valencia's orgasm sent Flo's body plummeting deliriously into her own well of pleasure. An urgent cry broke from her as the storm of joy rolled over them. The lovers clung to each other, the heat and intensity of the love and lust between them welding their bodies together.

After they cooled off, Valencia carefully pried herself away. Then, picking up her hat, she backed over to the door. She put her hat on and pulled it down low. Then, she gazed lovingly at Flo, who felt powerfully drawn and returned the look. Within seconds, Valencia turned and was gone.

IV

As Flo readied herself for the trip home the next morning, each task seemed harder to get through than the one before. She had no strength, and her body felt rubbery. Her head hurt from continuously crying. There was absolutely no pleasure in this leaving for her, not one redeeming quality. She wasn't missing anything from back home, and she already missed everything that she had come to love over the last week. Yet the course was laid out, she had only to follow it. And it took every bit of fortitude she had just to do that.

At the appointed hour she dragged her luggage over to the motel office, where the van would be picking up the group to drive them to Riverton Airport. From there a small propeller plane would take them to Denver, where they would each go their separate ways.

Most of Flo's mountain comrades were already waiting when she plopped her bag down and sat on it. Spirits were low; each one of them had fallen in love in one way or another with something about the place they were leaving. Flo was glad that she didn't have to make small talk. She simply didn't have it in her to fake feeling okay.

Lillie knew better than to offer to help. She knew there was nothing to be done and no words to be said that would make things any easier for Flo. All she could think of to do was to provide her with a hot cup of morning coffee, which she handed to her quietly, then moved to sit a few feet away. Flo accepted the coffee gratefully, but said nothing. She refused to look at Lill for fear that she would break down in tears. She sat, sipped, and let the morning sun soothe her.

When the van arrived, everyone piled in and settled themselves for the hour-long ride to Riverton Airport. Some chatting started among them as the stouter souls took on the job of trying to raise the spirits of the others. They had learned during the week that in group survival it was necessary for each person to share his or her strengths with the others, and likewise, be able to take from the strength of another. They had also learned about each other's emotional limits. They knew without knowing why, to give Flo a lot of space that morning. Flo stared out the window of the van as they rode along, letting her mind sink into nothingness.

When they reached the airport the little propeller plane was waiting. One by one they dropped off their luggage in the little terminal and passed through a door that opened to the runway. There, at the door, they each showed their tickets to a flight attendant before walking out to the plane. Flo was the last person in line. With her carry-on bag in hand, she pulled her ticket out of her pocket and made eye contact with the flight attendant. "Good morning," the woman greeted warmly. "Did you have a nice stay?"

Flo stared at her smiling eyes and said nothing. The woman repeated herself more loudly, as if she thought Flo might be hard of hearing. "Did you have a nice stay?" Flo kept staring at her dazedly. The flight attendant was becoming uncomfortable. She reached for Flo's ticket, which Flo held numbly in her hand. But when she tried to take it, Flo clamped down on it tightly with her fingers.

The flight attendant was now quite ill at ease, and her

smile was gone. She said, "Excuse me, miss, but are you taking this flight?"

Flo still said nothing.

Again, she asked, "Miss — are you taking this flight to Denver?"

Flo suddenly came to life. She smiled brightly and said, "No — No, I'm not. I'm sorry, I've made a mistake." Flo turned from the poor, bewildered woman and walked back through the little airport terminal and out the entrance. She walked around the building to a spot where she could see the Denver plane clearly and watched her wilderness family board it. As Lillie climbed the airplane steps, she turned her head and looked behind her, trying to locate Flo.

Flo cupped her mouth with her hands and yelled, "Lillie — over here!"

Lillie whipped her head around. Squinting her eyes, she finally found Flo standing next to the terminal building. "All right, Flo!" she cheered loudly. She made a fist and raised it into the air.

Flo returned the gesture.

"Write me!" Lillie yelled.

"Will do!" Flo answered.

Flo waited until she saw the plane lift off and take flight. Then she went back inside, found a pay phone, and called the number on the piece of paper that Valencia had given her. The phone rang for a long time. Flo began to worry that Valencia and the Chief were already out on their next trip. Finally, Valencia answered, her voice sounding hollow and dull.

"Valencia?" Tears rolled down Flo's cheeks.

"Flo?" Valencia said, tentatively. Then she shouted exuberantly, "Flo?!"

"I can't leave now," Flo blubbered. "If I do, I won't see Aussie grow up."

"Oh — God! Flo — really? Holy shit! Oh man!" Valencia was totally stunned. She paced rapidly back and forth, yanking the phone cord all around the room. "Where are you?"

"I'm at the airport."

"Oh no! Don't move. Don't get on anything. I'm on my way. Don't move! Flo?"

"I'll be waiting. I won't move an inch," Flo said reassuringly. "And Valencia?"

"What — what?" Valencia was still beside herself.

"Bring Aussie."

"Of course! We're on our way. I'm coming. I love you. I'm coming."